The Later Poetry
of Charlotte Perkins
Gilman

Charlotte Perkins Gilman. Photograph courtesy of Brown Brothers.

The Later Poetry
of Charlotte Perkins
Gilman

Edited by
Denise D. Knight

DELAWARE

Newark: University of Delaware Press
London: Associated University Presses

Associated University Presses
440 Forsgate Drive
Cranbury, NJ 08512

Associated University Presses
16 Barter Street
London WC1A 2AH, England

Associated University Presses
P.O. Box 338, Port Credit
Mississauga, Ontario
Canada L5G 4L8

The paper used in this publication meets the requirements
of the American National Standard for Permanence of Paper
for Printed Library Materials Z39.48–1984.

Library of Congress Cataloging-in-Publication Data

Gilman, Charlotte Perkins, 1860–1935.
     The later poetry of Charlotte Perkins Gilman / edited by Denise D. Knight.
          p.   cm.
     Includes bibliographical references.
     ISBN 0-87413-586-9 (alk. paper)
     I. Knight, Denise D., 1954–   .   II. Title.
     PS1744.G57A6   1996
     811'.4—dc20

96-3865
CIP

PRINTED IN THE UNITED STATES OF AMERICA

To Walter Stetson Chamberlin
and Linda Stetson Chamberlin

Contents

Part Two: The Philosopher

Part Three: The Artist

Up and Down

Up, up, up! On and out and away
   From the little beast I live in,
   From the sweet home life I give in,
     With its dear, close love;
Out of that fragrant gloom,
With its crowding fruit and bloom,
   Into the wide, clear day—
   Into the world above.

Out where the soul can spread
   Into the lives of many—
Feeling the joy and pain,
The peace, the toil, the strain
   That is not spared to any;
Feeling and working as one;
So is our life begun—
   The life that can never grow
   Till it has widened so.
The neighborless soul is dead.

Or—with a sharp-caught breath,
   Into a space beyond—
   Wonderful white-blue space,
Where you feel through shifting time
The slow-formed life sublime
   Of a yet unconscious race;
Where you live beyond all tears,
Where centuries slide as years,
And the flickering screen of death
   Shows God's face, calm and fond.

Even—a moment's dream—
   A flash that lifts and flies—
   Even beyond our brothers,
To a day when the full-born soul,

13

World-circling, conscious, whole,
  Shall taste the world's full worth—
  Shall feel the swing of the earth,
Feel what life will seem
  When we walk the thronging skies,
And the earth shall sing with the others.

Down, down, down! Back and in and home!
  Circling softly through
  The spaces vast and blue;
The centuries' whirling spokes
  Setting back again
  To time-marks clear and plain.
As we count the separate strokes,
  The race life-long and free
  Narrowed to what we see,
Our own set hope and power
In the history of the hour—
  Back to our time we come.

In, where the soul is warm
  With the clinging, lingering touch
  Of those we love so much,
And the daring wings can rest;
  Back where the task is small,
  Easy and plain to all,
The life that most hold best—
  Humanity's first form.

Down! If we fail of this;
  Down to the very base—
  The Universe, the Race,
Country and Friends and Home—
Here at the end we come
  To the first gift that was given,
  The little beast we live in!

Rest and be happy, soul!
This was an age-long goal—
  This, too, you may nobly love—
  Failing of aught above;
Feeling that even here,

Life is as true, as near,
  As one with the will of God,
  As sky or sea, or sod—
Or aught of the world that is.

CHARLOTTE PERKINS GILMAN

"Up and Down" was originally published in *Arena* 20 (October 1898): 478–79. In *The Living of Charlotte Perkins Gilman*, Gilman characterized "Up and Down" as "quite the highest and farthest I ever reached" (246). The placement of "Up and Down" as the opening poem in this edition is Amy Wellington's, as cited in correspondence dated 5 August 1935, folder 125, Gilman Papers, Schlesinger Library, Radcliffe College.

A Note on the Text

In compiling the 167 poems included in this edition of *THE LATER Poetry of Charlotte Perkins Gilman*, I have retained the three divisions planned by Gilman's friend and editor Amy Wellington: "The Satirist," "The Philosopher," and "The Artist." Except for the specific placement of six poems mentioned by Wellington in extant correspondence, which I have also retained—"Up and Down," "A Central Sun," "Worship," "Wings," "The Grapevine," and "California Colors"—there is no mention of the order planned by Wellington for the remaining poems. If Wellington completed a table of contents, it has not survived as part of the Gilman Papers.

Often, individual poems could be classified in two or even more ways. To the extent possible, however, I have classified the poems by their most prominent features and have attempted to arrange the works within each section by grouping poems with similar themes. Because many of the poems are undated, a chronological arrangement was not possible.

Poems were initially transcribed from microfiche and later verified against the original manuscripts contained in folders 186–94 of the Gilman Papers at the Schlesinger Library at Radcliffe College. Gilman's capitalization, spelling, punctuation, indentations, and underlinings have been preserved. The only liberty I have taken is in the list of poems in the appendix, where I eliminated duplicate titles and corrected misnumberings. Original publication dates for previously published works, and any other marginal notations placed on the manuscript copy by Gilman, are documented in the notes.

Acknowledgments

I WISH TO RECOGNIZE THE FOLLOWING INDIVIDUALS AND INSTITUTIONS for rendering assistance during the preparation of this manuscript: Eva S. Moseley, Acting Director of the Schlesinger Library at Radcliffe College, deserves thanks for her early support of this project. I also wish to thank Earline Sorensen, Special Projects Coordinator at the National Women's Hall of Fame in Seneca Falls, New York, for helping me to locate the photograph of Gilman included in this edition. Gretchen Gogan from the Interlibrary Loan Department at the State University of New York College at Cortland was extremely helpful in responding to my requests for information. For financial support, I wish to thank the Schlesinger Library at Radcliffe College for awarding me a 1994–95 Research Support Grant. The English Department at the State University of New York at Cortland deserves thanks for allowing me a course reduction during the Spring 1994 semester so that I could devote more time to this project. I am also grateful to Gary Scharnhorst for his support and particularly for publishing an essay on Gilman's later poetry, which inspired me to resume work on this project after putting it aside several years earlier. Special thanks to my sister, Cindy J. Hall, for sharing my enthusiasm about Gilman's life and literature. And finally, I thank my husband, Michael K. Barylski, for his unqualified and enduring support of my work.

Introduction

Denise D. Knight

In her review of the posthumously published autobiography, *The Living of Charlotte Perkins Gilman*, (*Saturday Review*, 20 June 1936), feminist author Amy Wellington characterized Gilman as "unquestionably the most extraordinary New England woman of her day, the most original thinker, the most powerful speaker and writer."[1] Wellington recalled not only the numerous "sociological studies" that Gilman had written, but she also alluded to her long-time friend's final work, a book of verse titled *Here Also*. "These poems," Wellington remarked, "written in the leisure hours of an arduous life, are the full-flowering of Charlotte Gilman's philosophy."

Indeed, this edition, which was to have been Gilman's second volume of published verse, offers the full range of her poetic voice by featuring satire, philosophical verse, nature poetry, and light verse. Despite Gilman's attempts to arrange for its publication in the final months of her life, however, the manuscript has remained unpublished until now.

Born in 1860 into the politically progressive Beecher family of New England (her father was the nephew of Harriet Beecher Stowe and Henry Ward Beecher), Charlotte Anna Perkins formed a philosophy that would govern her life from an early age. "The first duty of a human being is to . . . find our places, our special work in the world, and when found, do it, do it at all costs," she explained in her autobiography.[2] It was a philosophy that Gilman embraced. After the end of her turbulent ten-year marriage to American artist Charles Walter Stetson, during which she suffered a nervous breakdown following the birth of her daughter, Katharine, Gilman immersed herself in work and emerged as one of the intellectual leaders of the turn-of-the-century women's movement. Her work was shaped by her belief in the need for social reform, by her advocacy of nationalism in the 1890s, and particularly by her support of Reform Darwinism. An influential social theorist and champion of women's economic independence, Gilman became an enormously prolific writer. At the age of thirty-three, she published her first book, a highly acclaimed volume of poetry titled *In This Our World* (1893), and

21

in 1898, at the age of thirty-eight, her landmark work, *Women and Economics* garnered international attention and was quickly translated into seven languages. Several other nonfiction books followed: *Concerning Children* (1900), *The Home: Its Work and Influence* (1903), *Human Work* (1904), *The Man-Made World; Or, Our Androcentric Culture* (1911) and *His Religion and Hers* (1923). Novels were published separately, and serially, in *Forerunner*, a monthly magazine that Gilman singlehandedly wrote and published between 1909–16, which also featured nearly 125 of her short stories and hundreds of her poems. Gilman became a world-renowned lecturer, and her work was praised by such prominent figures as William Dean Howells, Upton Sinclair, Jane Addams, Lester F. Ward, and Carrie Chapman Catt, who ranked Gilman first in her list of "America's Twelve Greatest Women."[3] Only in the last ten years of Gilman's life did her public visibility decline. She lamented in her autobiography that "after so many years of work for the advancement of women . . . and with so much that was new and strong to say to the coming generation," her services as a speaker were no longer in demand (*Living* 333). In 1932, Gilman learned that she had breast cancer, and in 1934, her second husband, George Houghton Gilman, whom she had married in 1900 at the age of thirty-nine, died suddenly from a cerebral hemorrhage. At the age of seventy-five, and suffering the effects of the disease, Gilman concluded that it was "the simplest of human rights to choose a quick and easy death in place of a slow and horrible one" (*Living* 333). For several months, Gilman carefully planned her suicide, and on 17 August 1935, she ended her life.[4]

Although she grew increasingly weak during the final stage of her three-year battle with cancer, Gilman's resolve to see her second book of poetry in print never diminished. In the author's note at the beginning of her autobiography, Gilman thanked Wellington, a "keen but gentle critic," for having arranged her "second book of poems, *Here Also*" (*Living* xxv). Even as late as just twelve days before Gilman's suicide, Wellington was responding by letter to Gilman's suggestions about the order in which the poems should appear. "The work on the poems is almost completed, and I hope you will like my introduction," she wrote to Gilman. "I rearranged the poems exactly according to your plan, and consider it a far better one than my own. . . . I shall send a type-written copy of the 'Contents' of 'Here Also!' for your criticism,"[5] Wellington promised. Her introduction and table of contents are not among the Gilman Papers owned by the Schlesinger Library at Radcliffe College, however, making it unlikely that they were sent, if, indeed, they were ever even written.

In his essay, "Reconstructing *Here Also*: On the Later Poetry of Charlotte Perkins Gilman,"[6] Gary Scharnhorst speculates that Wellington's inability to secure a publisher for Gilman's new collection of poems "may, in the end, be explained simply by the radically discordant tones among them" (258). Indeed, extant correspondence suggests that both Gilman and Wellington struggled with the structure and arrangement of the volume. "There is so much diversity in your poems that it is quite a little feat to place them all together without sharp or awkward changes," Wellington noted in one of her last letters to Gilman.[7] After experimenting with various configurations, Wellington finally decided to divide the volume into three sections: "The Satirist," "The Philosopher," and "The Artist." "The poems naturally separate themselves into three sections," she wrote on 5 May 1935. As Scharnhorst points out, the planned division of poems would "mirror the tripartite structure" of Gilman's highly successful volume of verse, *In This Our World*, published in four editions between 1893 and 1898 (250).

While careful arrangement of the poems would eliminate some of those "sharp or awkward changes" that concerned Wellington, other factors also seem likely to have impeded publication. Foremost among them was the physical condition of the manuscript, which consisted simply of a folder of loose poems, many still in Gilman's hand. Gilman herself was acutely aware that the collection in its present state was not acceptable for publication consideration. To her cousin and literary executor, Lyman Beecher Stowe (Harriet's grandson), she confided her concern and irreverently suggested that after her death, in lieu of flowers, he pay his respects by financing the typing of the poetry manuscript: "I meant to have prepared for Miss Wellington a nicely typed set of poems—! Not strong enough. Do you think (instead of "flowers"!) you and Hilda could help in having them typed?"[8] Although Stowe had knowledge of Gilman's suicide plans and was willing to offer some financial assistance in her final weeks, there were limits to his generosity. On 4 June 1935, he agreed to "pay for the typing" of the poems but added that "if it's a considerable amount [I] will perhaps ask reimbursement out of royalties."[9] Just three weeks later, however, he was feeling somewhat less charitable: "Could you afford to pay for the typing of the poems out of the $250.00 advance [from *The Living of Charlotte Perkins Gilman*]? If so instruct Mr. Wing [Gilman's literary agent] that he may send you the bill."[10] Gilman's reply was terse: "Of course I [will] pay for typing the poems! And any other necessary bills."[11] The volume, however, was apparently never typed.

There is considerable doubt, in fact, as to whether or not Amy Wellington ever actually wrote an introduction to the collection or whether her allusions to it were intended simply to comfort a dying friend who desperately wanted the world to remember her. There is some evidence to support the latter scenario.

Indeed, during the final months before her suicide on 17 August 1935, Gilman placed considerable demands on various friends and relatives in her drive to get her works published. Despite her declining health, or perhaps because of it, Gilman's sense of urgency remained strong. Her long-time friend, Pulitzer-prize-winning author Zona Gale (1874–1938), was less than enthusiastic when asked by Gilman to write her biography. Immersed in her own writing projects, Gale declined Gilman's request. Gilman persisted, however, and although she complained to Lyman Beecher Stowe that Gale had spent "a mere half hour!"[12] talking to her about the project, Gale eventually agreed to contribute a foreword to Gilman's autobiography. In June 1935, with Gilman's death just weeks away, Gale persuaded the Appleton-Century Company to issue a contract for *The Living of Charlotte Perkins Gilman* without delay.[13]

Once Gilman was reasonably certain that the autobiography would be published, she renewed her efforts to prepare the volume of verse for publication. To Wellington she wrote, "Maybe later they'll get out some 'miscellany'—maybe I'll never achieve this 'revival' at all! Anyway, send the stuff back to Lyman—what you don't use. The main thing of course is the real book—'Gilman's Poems.'"[14] Lyman Beecher Stowe was also inundated by requests from Gilman to follow through on the various efforts to get her later work published.[15]

While Amy Wellington and Lyman Beecher Stowe tried to be supportive, both also attempted to gently impress upon Gilman that there were other demands on their time. Wellington, in particular, was often plagued by the aftereffects of an illness that nearly caused her death several years earlier.[16] Still, she promised Gilman that she would make the editing of the poetry her top priority. On 16 April 1935, she wrote, "I shall drop everything and devote myself to the poems, with the one thought in mind of placing the new volume in your hands as quickly as possible." On 5 May, however, Wellington noted that her progress had been "interrupted by one of [her] unfortunate illnesses" but reassured Gilman that she would complete the project before Gilman's death.[17] "[I] will not give up my unshaken faith that you will be with us much longer than you think—that we shall place the new book of poems in your dear hands." But on 3 July 1935, there is both an implicit apology and a subtle attempt to obviate any impatience on Gilman's part. "Dearest Charlotte," the letter reads, . . . "I've been ill again. That is why you have not heard from me." Two weeks later, on 17 July: "I am tremendously enthusiastic about this collection of Poems and do not mind my little illnesses, dear Charlotte, unless they are incapacitating— There's so much to do, so little time in which to do it!"

The problem of time did, indeed, loom large in Wellington's mind, both from the perspective that Gilman's health was rapidly deteriorating and Wellington's own illnesses delayed her work. When Lyman Beecher Stowe and literary agent Willis Kingsley Wing, who was attempting to place the poetry with a publisher, insisted that Wellington incorporate a biographical sketch of Gilman into the introduction,[18] the pressure on Wellington became enormous. Several weeks later, Wellington was still struggling to get it written. Her 12 June 1935 letter to Gilman betrays her ambivalence about the introduction: "I have been deep in biographical matter this morning, as both Mr. Stowe and Mr. Wing are very urgent about such an introduction to the poems—and probably they are right. The book is so powerful, however, so shining and beautiful, that one hesitates to be intrusive, even with a foreword." And less than a month later, Wellington admitted trying to nix the plans for an introduction altogether:

> When I heard of the Fall publication of the Autobiography, I called up Mr. Wing and suggested that a biographical introduction to the Poems was unnecessary—he did not agree with me. Both he and Mr. Stowe have been urgent in the matter of biographical detail—This, of course, has taken more time than the short simple foreword I had planned. You know the slowness with which I write—and here I am particularly anxious that every word should be worthy of the subject.[19]

Two weeks later, Wellington again purported to be hard at work on the edition: "Dearest Charlotte! Whenever I feel like writing to you (and that is very often!), the Poems look sternly at me—and doesn't Mr. W. Wordsworth tell us that 'stern duty is the voice of God'?"[20] Yet, she was still quietly complaining about having to tailor the introduction to meet the specifications of Stowe and Wing: "I'll keep sufficiently to the biographical in my introduction—though I think Mr. Stowe and Mr. Wing are biographically bitten. They all are today," she lamented.

The loose, largely untyped folder of poems that Wellington eventually returned to the "biographically bitten" Lyman Beecher Stowe, however, following Gilman's death, contains no introduction to the intended edition, further suggesting that it was never written. Wellington knew that Gilman's planned "exit," as she referred to her suicide, was imminent, and both she and Stowe probably viewed the publication of the autobiography as far more urgent than the volume of poetry. Once the autobiography was accepted for publication in June, 1935—an event that pleased Gilman enormously—it alleviated the immediate pressure on Wellington and Stowe to secure a publisher for the verse as well. It is also likely that neither one wished to bear the expense of having the poetry manuscript properly prepared.[21]

While it is not clear for how long or to what extent Amy Wellington and Willis K. Wing attempted to market the poetry, Appleton-Century had declined the project within two weeks after Gilman's death.[22] Correspondence indicates that there had been some discussion, at Gilman's urging, about issuing a two-volume edition of the poetry by reprinting the highly successful *In This Our World* as volume one and appending *Here Also* as volume two, but those plans apparently fell by the wayside, as suggested by Gilman's allusion to the one-volume edition of *Here Also* in the autobiography (*Living* xxv). Gilman's daughter, Katharine Beecher Chamberlin, still held some hope that the poems would be placed after her mother's death, and her disappointment over their nonpublication is apparent in extant correspondence. In a letter to Lyman Beecher Stowe dated 11 January 1936, Katharine wrote: "[I have received] another letter from some one wanting to buy poems. I do wish they were out. I believe more would sell than of anything else she has written." And in July 1936, Katharine suggested to Stowe that the more receptive audience in England, where Gilman had enjoyed a "far higher reputation than at home" (*Living* 201), might be the right market in which to launch the new edition. "I observe that 'In This Our World' was published in England before Small & Maynard brought it out. It does seem as if Miss Wellington's suggestion of following up the English end was sound. It seems as if the poems ought to come out while the interest holds," she wrote.[23] Instead, they remained in Katharine's possession until the Gilman Papers were acquired by Radcliffe College in the early 1970s.

* * *

"Dearest Charlotte," Wellington wrote on 5 May 1935, "There is no doubt about the power and beauty—and the *timeliness* of this second volume of your poems, which about equals in size the first. . . . [24] Am trying to keep in mind always what you would desire and approve while—at the same time—thinking of your readers." Two months later, Wellington was still assigning poems into various categories, and extant correspondence provides an occasional glimpse of her tentative arrangement of at least some of the poems: "I placed that magnificent 'Gunman' with the satires, because—speaking largely—it *is* a satire, isn't it? Your philosophic poems are sometimes didactic, and the didacticism is always philosophic, so I had no trouble in classifying here," Wellington wrote on 3 July 1935. "And somehow it satisfied my sense of the fitting to put the philosophy between those dynamic satires and all the loveliness, beginning with 'Wings' and ending with 'California Colors.'"

In fact, Wellington had her work cut out for her. Although Gilman had compiled a tentative table of contents for her second volume of verse, dated 12 February 1935, the list contained duplicate entries, errors in numbering, and incomplete or inaccurate titles (see Appendix). As

Scharnhorst observes, "it is now impossible to know for a certainty which poems on Gilman's list Wellington planned to assign to each category. She continually rearranged the order of works within each section, it seems" (250). Further complicating Wellington's task was Gilman's frequent instructions to Wellington to include additional poems. At times, Gilman's own ambivalence over what to include and what not to must have caused Wellington enormous frustration. "Dear Amy," Gilman wrote on 5 April 1935. "I don't know what to say about the nonsense verse. . . . 'The Dream of Gold,' albeit nonsense is good poetry. 'The Melancholy Rabbit' is a gem—if I did do it." But Gilman's indecision on one day might be followed by explicit instructions on another. "All your instructions concerning the poems are carefully noted," Wellington wrote to Gilman on 16 April 1935. "When any question arises, I shall write for your decision," she promised. Unfortunately, few of Gilman's responses to Wellington's inquiries have survived, so it is impossible to know her reaction to her "keen but gentle critic['s]" suggestions and queries.

* * *

Gilman's love of poetry began during her childhood in Providence, Rhode Island. "Poetry was always a delight to me," she remarked in her autobiography (*Living* 28). She not only committed "miles of it" to memory but began composing her own verses at an early age. "At sixteen, I wrote the first bit of verse that seemed to me real poetry, a trifling thing about white violets," she recalled (*Living* 70). While that poem and another early verse—an apostrophe to dandelion greens—[25] celebrated the beauty of nature, it wasn't long before Gilman's verses became politicized. Two of her earliest published poems, in fact, addressed the oppression of women. One, "In Duty, Bound," written shortly before her marriage to Walter Stetson in 1884, depicts the "weary life" and "wasting power" that women confront when they sacrifice their individualism in marriage. The other, "One Girl of Many," reprinted here, is a sympathetic portrait of prostitution, in which Gilman chronicles the events that lead young women into a life of "dishonor," "misery," and "sin." Gilman saw an analogy between women who were "exploited for the pleasure of men, not only in prostitution, but also in their helpless subservience in marriage."[26] Like virtually everything that Gilman wrote, poetry became yet another vehicle through which to advance her social theories.

Significantly, Cheryl Walker notes that the typical woman poet of Gilman's generation "was expected to confirm prevailing social values" and not to "provide serious political, social, or religious challenges to the status quo."[27] Gilman's heavily didactic poetry, however, marks a clear departure from the norm. "I don't call it a book of poems," Gilman remarked in 1896, after *In This Our World* appeared in a second edition. "I call it a tool box. It was written to drive nails with."[28] Even her first husband, Walter Stetson, complained about the didacticism in her verse: "I confess I wish she'd strive more for beauty in poetry than for didactics, for when she does let herself forget to preach she writes very very tender & lovely things," he remarked.[29]

Although Gilman preferred to write "nail-driving" poetry, she enjoyed reading the more artistic works of such poets as Elizabeth Barrett Browning, Christina Rossetti, Rudyard Kipling, Jean Ingelow, Oliver Wendell Holmes, and Henry Wadsworth Longfellow. She was also personally acquainted with California poets Ina Coolbrith, Joaquin Miller, and Edwin Markham. Her favorite poet, however, was Walt Whitman.[30] In 1891, Gilman publicly hailed Whitman as "America's greatest poet,"[31] and a few years later, Whitman's *Leaves of Grass* was one of only two books that Gilman carried with her during a two-year lecture tour.[32] Despite her deep and abiding admiration of Whitman's sensual free verse, artistry in her own poetry remained secondary to the message. "I am not a poet," she insisted. "I'm only a preacher, whether on the platform or in print."[33] Clearly, Gilman valued the didactic power of her verse.

As a poet, Gilman's strongest work was, arguably, her satirical verse. Her most famous poem, a satire on social conservatism titled "Similar Cases," first published in 1890, was praised by numerous critics, including William Dean Howells, with whom Gilman would become friends in later years. Howells wrote Gilman that he had "read it many times with unfailing joy," (*Living* 113) and Gilman's uncle, prominent Unitarian clergyman and author, Edward Everett Hale, hailed "Similar Cases" as a "great campaign document" for Nationalism (*Living* 129). American editor, novelist and playwright Floyd Dell was even more enthusiastic, characterizing Gilman as author of "the best satirical verses of modern times."[34] And Horace L. Traubel, Whitman's close friend and literary executor, offered exceptionally warm praise of Gilman's first volume of poetry, *In This Our World,* in an 1898 review.[35]

The satirical verses collected in Part 1 of this edition showcase Gilman's talent as a lampoonist of various social issues. The topics cover a wide range—the evolution versus creation debate, the pervasiveness of yellow journalism, the meat-packing scandal in the early part of the twentieth century, America's role in World War I, the limitations imposed by women's clothing, the influx of immigrants into the United States, the myopic existence of the turn-of-the-century housewife—and each poem bears the distinctive imprint of Gilman's satirical bite.

"Her civic satire is of a form which she has herself invented; it recalls the work of no one else," Howells remarked of Gilman's verse in the *North American Review* in 1899.[36] He observed that while "no satire approaching it in the wit flashing from profound conviction"[37] had appeared since the publication of James Russell Lowell's *Biglow Papers* in 1848, "the implications of her satire are for social reform of a very radical kind" and that it would not appeal to those who "cannot enjoy . . . very witty criticisms of our conditions."[38] Indeed, in both volumes of poetry, Gilman used her satirical verse to advance her position on some of the same social, political, and economic issues about which she frequently wrote and lectured. Her promotion of ethical journalism, for example, was developed through such forums as essays, lectures, editorials, and even fiction. In three satirical poems on the topic, "The War-Skunk," "Hyenas," and "The Yellow Reporter," Gilman castigated newspaper journalists who resorted to unscrupulous methods to obtain a story. Likewise, four of her satirical verses address both the economic impact and the public health risk associated with the meat-packing scandal in the early part of the twentieth century in which adulterated food was distributed and sold. Another poem, "We Eat at Home," promotes Gilman's advocacy of the "kitchenless home," an architectural innovation she advanced in such works as *Women and Economics* and *The Home*. The kitchenless home, Gilman argued, would help to free women from domestic oppression by shifting the most time-consuming household duty outside of the home and into the hands of professional chefs.

In a more serious vein, Gilman betrayed her intolerance of a multiethnic society in her highly metaphorical satire, "The Melting Pot," in which she dismissed as "swill" the "queer mixture" of nationalities that resulted from the absence of a more restrictive U.S. immigration policy. The poem echoes the xenophobic sentiments expressed in her autobiography in which she bitterly lamented that New York City, her home for twenty-two years, had become an "unnatural city where everyone is an exile, none more so than the American" (*Living* 316). In another dark satire titled "Why? To the United States of America, 1915–1916," Gilman blasted the U.S. government for its failure to render immediate assistance to its allies during World War I. Another war poem, "On Germany," betrays Gilman's contempt for Germany's role in the war in every line.

Satirical humor was also invoked by Gilman in addressing more banal matters. In response to "the callous indifference of speakers to the rights of others," for example—a problem she frequently encountered on the lecture circuit—Gilman wrote a "bit of caustic verse."[39] Titled "The Speaker's Sin," the poem derides those long-winded, egotistical speakers who monopolize the podium in public forums. She also used humor to

ridicule impractical women's fashions, from her "ugly hat" to her crip-
pling shoes, in a half dozen poems. While the acceptance of Gilman's
"humor and sarcasm" might be "confined to fanatics, philanthropists and
other Dangerous Persons," Howells noted in the *North American Review*,
"that need not keep us from owning its brilliancy."[40]

Among the works collected in Part 2 of this volume, "The Philoso-
pher," are several poems in which Gilman advances her theories about
human nature and the responsibility incumbent upon individuals to
effect positive change. "Human virtue and human happiness are matters
of cause and effect," she lectured in 1890.[41] "*Through* and *by* the laws
of nature must all good come, and we must learn those laws and follow
them," she insisted. Indeed, in such works as "The Fatalist and The
Sailorman," "Tree & Sun," "The Earth, The World, and I," and "The
Kingdom," Gilman dramatizes a host of philosophical issues, including
the effect of heredity versus environment, the sources of women's oppres-
sion, and her steadfast confidence in the inevitability of progress.

In "The Rabbit, The Rhinoceros & I," for example, Gilman's belief in
the ability of human beings to alter their condition is clearly illustrated.
Likewise, in "Why Nature Laughs," Gilman suggests that society alone
is responsible for its sorry state. "Grandma Nature," who assumes the
role of the philosopher in this verse, explains that men and women have
invited much of their grief upon themselves:

> You hedge yourselves with needless walls,
>   You bind with needless chains,
> You drive away your natural joys,
>   And court unnatural pains.

Yet humans, according to Nature, foolishly fail to seek solutions to the
"hell" they have created. Similarly in the poem, "Begin Now," Gilman
insists that "the world we want is for us to make."

Also collected in Part 2 are several clever apothegms including "The
Daily Squid," "The Front Wave," and "Queer People," as well as poems
that emphasize the value of such human characteristics as truth, courage,
love, joy, and power. "Two Prayers" and "Between Past & Future," for
example, both celebrate the joy of self-empowerment. Several other
works in this section develop the tension between dichotomous elements:
youth and age, old and new, past and present. Another poem, "Good
Will," was written after Gilman had escaped "the foulest misrepresenta-
tion and abuse [she had] ever known" (*Living* 180), as a result of public
condemnation following her divorce in 1894.[42] The poem serves as a
self-reminder not to waste sorrow "on the days that lie behind" or to
waste fear on "days that rise before."

Poems written for and about women are also featured in this section. While fewer in number than in any edition of *In This Our World*, the poems about women address some of Gilman's foremost concerns: economic disparity between the sexes, subservience in the home, and women's suffrage. Some of the selections are upbeat in their call for solidarity, as in "A Chant Royal" and "Happy Day." Other poems, such as "To the Indifferent Woman," admonish housewives in particular not to become so removed from the world at large that they forget that "The one first duty of all human life / Is to promote the progress of the world." Other works, such as "Full Motherhood," address Gilman's idea of the "new motherhood," which advocated "the fullest development of the woman, in all her powers, that she may be better qualified for her [maternal] duties."[43] And one poem, titled "Body of Mine," is an affirmation of old age: while the once "soft, smooth, and fair" body has grown "thin, dry, and old," the speaker's soul is "Young forever to all demands / Ageless and deathless and boundless and free." Occasionally, Gilman's poetry about women assumes a dark tone, as in the early verse, "One Girl of Many," discussed previously.

The poetry featured in Part 3, "The Artist," is more varied and less didactic than that contained in Parts 1 and 2. Featuring poems about nature, children's verse, nonsense poetry, and occasional verse, the selections featured in Part 3 span fifty-four years of Gilman's life, from "My View, 1881" to her last-known poem, "The Grapevine," written in March 1935, just five months prior to her death.

Although Gilman "never made any pretense of being literary" (*Living* 284) and preferred to subordinate artistry to didacticism, several of the poems in this section reveal her artistic side. Gilman was capable of "making pure and beautiful poetry," Wellington observed, and although she was not "given to the luxury of self-expression . . . the passion for beauty" is present in her verse.[44] Still, the didacticism is implicit: the role of the artist, Gilman wrote, is to act as "the intermediate lens / Of God, and so best gives Him to the world / Intensified, interpreted to us."[45]

In addition to the transcendental contemplations that one sees in such poems as "Wings" and "Worship," several of the selections in Part 3 celebrate the simple beauty of nature. "I am poet enough to know that the natural world is divine and the divine world is natural," Gilman wrote in 1891.[46] She particularly enjoyed writing poems about the California landscape, several of which are included in this edition. "California always makes me sing," she noted on one of the poems she sent to Amy Wellington.[47] One of the "spatters" of California verse, as Gilman referred to her "Little Flutters of California Beauty," is striking in its simplicity:

> Long lines of eucalyptus run, an endless race, an
>   easy grace,
> Free verse in living green.

Gilman was also pleased with her poem, "Santa Barbara to San Jose."
"Be sure this goes [in]," she instructed Amy Wellington in 1935. "I
love it."[48]

One other group of poems in this section, "River Windows," was
written around 1910 when Gilman lived in New York City. "There was
a huge boulder, quite near us, where people used to sit and watch the
sun set, as if it were in the country; trees that we could lie under and
look at the stars," she explained in her autobiography (*Living* 295–96).
"The sheer beauty of [it] so filled me that I began to write poetry about
it, a descriptive set, called 'River Windows.'" Gilman hoped to publish
the poems, but those hopes "were not shared by editors" (*Living* 296).

Gilman also thought that "Mer-Songs," a delightful collection of chil-
dren's verse included in "The Artist," might be published as a separate
book. Despite the encouragement of an editor, who suggested that she
"give [her]self" over to the writing of children's verses since she obviously
"had a special talent for it" (*Living* 161), "Mer-Songs" also remained
unpublished. Another child's verse, "The Bad Little Coo-Bird," was writ-
ten for her daughter Katharine in 1891.[49]

In addition to the children's poems, Part 3 contains several examples
of Gilman's nonsense verse, sometimes written in collaboration with
others. So titled because they consist of poetic absurdities, the nonsense
verse collected in this edition includes "A Walk, Walk, Walk," "Aunt
Eliza," "Chilly Weather," "A Dream of Gold," and "The Melancholy
Rabbit." Both the children's verse and the nonsense verse reveals Gil-
man's playful side and offers an intriguing contrast to her dark political
satires. Although correspondence reveals that Gilman felt some ambiva-
lence about whether to include the nonsense verse in the second volume
of poetry, there is nothing to suggest that either she or Wellington decided
to remove it.

Several of Gilman's occasional poems are included in this section.
One of her favorites, the previously unpublished "On a Tub of Butter,
Christmas 1882," was preserved by Gilman for nearly fifty-three years.
Unlike the majority of her poems, "On a Tub of Butter" is unrhymed and
contains a Whitmanesque catalog of evocative pastoral images. Other
occasional poems include a birthday tribute to a long-time friend and a
verse written "For a Guest Book."

Also included in "The Artist" is a particularly fine tribute to the Ameri-
can dancer, Isadora Duncan. Gilman attended a performance by Dun-
can in 1915 and wrote in the *Forerunner* that "the beauty one sees in

[her] dancing" is "so lovely, so penetrating in its appeal that it brings tears to the eyes and 'a lump in the throat'—the whole soul is lit and lifted by it."[50] The simple artistry and casual elegance of "To Isadora Duncan" sets it apart from several of the other poems in this section; Gilman has effectively captured in the lines of this poem the graceful beauty of Duncan's dancing.

* * *

In her final months of life, Charlotte Perkins Gilman feared that she would be forgotten. She would unquestionably be pleased by the ongoing revival of her work and the renewed interest in her life.[51] In 1993, a study conducted by the Siena Research Institute named Gilman sixth in their list of the "Ten Most Influential Women of the Twentieth Century." And in 1994, the National Women's Hall of Fame in Seneca Falls, New York paid Gilman the ultimate tribute by inducting her into their ranks.

A few weeks before her death, Amy Wellington tried to assure Gilman that her words and wisdom would, indeed, be preserved for future generations. Her poetry and other works, Wellington wrote to Gilman, "are for the new time coming! Not for yesterday, but for tomorrow!"[52] Some sixty years after her death, *The Later Poetry of Charlotte Perkins Gilman*—her final work—can serve as an enduring reminder of her convictions, her passion, and her indomitable spirit.

The Later Poetry
of Charlotte Perkins Gilman

Part One
The Satirist

THE SON OF BOTH

"Man is the son of the Ape,"
  The scientists say—
"The same immutable laws
That have given the crab his claws,
To the fish his shimmering scale,
And the whalebone to the whale,
Feathery wings to birds,
Horns to the grazing herds—
Preparing each for strife
With the elements of life—
Have lifted Man's proud neck
From the protoplasmic speck,
Builded in ceaseless time
From the warm, primeval slime;
So came his wonderful brain
From ages of stress and strain,
So came his wonderful shape—
Man is the son of the Ape!"
  The Scientists say.

"Man is the son of God,"
  The Ministers say—
The Universal Soul
Which filleth the mighty whole
And each invisible part
Filleth the human heart;
And every bird and beast
From the greatest to the least
Was made by God's right hand
For Man's supreme command;
Each strange and beautiful sight
Created for his delight;
All that is ripe and sweet
So ordered for him to eat.
Out of the sinless Whole
Cometh the sinful soul—
Divinity shut in a clod—

Man is the son of God!"
    The ministers say.

The Scientists say
"All Man's folly and crime
Are regular fruits of Time,
Following without pause
The same immutable laws.
Vain is the struggle, vain,
With sin and sorrow and pain;
Steadily, out of the dust
Man climbs, because he must.
Slowly, with Time's release,
Cometh the age of peace;
No conscious struggle of man
Can hasten the mighty plan.
Let him be still and bow
To Law that reigneth now;
Suffer, be still, and die,
Waiting for by and by.
All man's folly and crime
Are regular fruits of Time,"
    The Scientists say.

The Ministers say,
"This life of labor and dole
Is the punishment of the soul
For the soul's original sin;
Man must ever begin
From the cradle and the breast
A struggle that has no rest;
A single-handed fight
Against this world's delight;
A never-ending strife
With all the joys bf life,
While God shines on his throne
And the Devil claims his own;
By his own might and God's grace
He must fight for a higher place;
From the cradle to the grave
He must wrestle his soul to save.
This life of labor and dole

Is the punishment of the soul!"
  The Ministers say.

Whoso heedeth the one
Hath no joy under the sun.
He findeth this world a fetter
That keepeth him from a better;
He liveth in endless din
Of strife and shame and sin
And doeth naught to mend it,
But waiteth for Death to end it.
Whoso heedeth the other
Calleth the worm his brother;
He findeth this world a fetter
And believeth there is no better;
He liveth in endless din
Of strife and shame and sin,
And doeth naught to mend it
But waiteth for Time to end it.

Helpless product of Law—
What is thy Reason for?—
Why art thou helpless still?
Where is the Human Will.
Boundless, exhaustless, free,
Based on Divinity?
Pitiful prey of sin—
Hast thou no brain within?
Canst thou not learn at last
Out of the groaning past
That thy mad woes have cause
In Nature's broken laws?
Fool, the son of the Ape!
Sinner, the son of God!
Spirit, in earth-born shape!
Beast in a soul-filled clod!
Child of a wondrous birth,
Link between Heaven and Earth,
Creature of crime and sloth—
Thou art the son of Both!

CHILD LABOR [NO. 1]

The human race has risen
  By the love its children know,
By the length of human childhood,
  Fed and bred and sheltered so.

Time of freedom, time of playing,
  Time to grow in all that's true;
Time to reach a nobler manhood
  Than their parents ever knew.

Care and labor laid on children
  Robs our childhood of its place;
And the injury of childhood
  Is the ruin of the race.

Weakened, aged prematurely
  Low in virtue, less in size,
The race that works its children
  Eats itself, and surely dies.

CHILD LABOR [NO. 2]

The children in the Poor House
  May die of many an ill,
But the Poor House does not profit
  By their labor in the mill.

The children in the Orphanage
  Wear raiment far from fine,
But no Orphanage is financed
  By child labor in a mine.

Only the loving family
  Which we so much admire
Is willing to support itself
  By little children's hire.

Only the human father,
  A man, with power to think,

42

Will take from little children
    The price of food and drink.

Only the human mother,
    Degraded helpless thing,
Will make her little children work
    And live on what they bring.

No fledgling feeds the father-bird,
    No chicken feeds the hen,
No kitten mouses for the cat,
    This glory is for men.

We are the wisest strongest race,
    Long may our praise be sung,
The only animal alive
    That feeds upon its young.

We make the poverty that takes
    The lives of children so,
We can awake, rebuild, remake,
    And let our children grow.

EN BANC

Associate Justices of Court Supreme!
    Stern arbiters of destiny in law!
Thy gathered dignity and power would seem
    August a thing as people ever saw.

Associate Justices of Court Supreme!
    Sitting *en banc* to punish for contempt;
To see you sitting, who would ever dream
    That you from such opinion were exempt?

A crowded room with vulgar men who spit—
    Spit on the crimson carpet without shame.
This before Justice—in the sight of it—
    The highest thing for which we have a name!

Then "Hear ye! Hear ye! Hear ye!" is the cry,
  We rise, they shamble in, the court room stares,
While these great Justices *en banc* go by
  And take possession of their rocking-chairs.

Their rocking-chairs. Their cane-backed rocking-chairs!
  Wherein they swing and dandle to and fro,
Lounging and stretching has lazy airs
  As smoking-rooms and billiard parlors know.

Grave issues hang on every spoken word,
  The people listen, whispering in pairs,
The case proceeds, and through it all is heard
  The steady squeaking of their rocking-chairs.

How can we honor Justice when 'tis seen
  In men who shame her temple (or her tomb),
Who can insult the Goddess with a mien
  That would debar them from a drawing-room?

No reverence is too deep from those who claim
  The highest ground that mortal soul has trod;
Those who serve Justice, standing in her name,
  Serve in the presence of the living God.

A PSALM OF LIVES
(WITH APOLOGIES TO LONGFELLOW.)

They tell now us in mystic numbers
  Life is all a Freudian dream,
For the soul is safe that slumbers—
  Things are worse than what they seem.

Life is sex; in life thou burnest,
  In the grave a smouldering coal,
Lust thou art to lust returnest
  They are writing of the soul.

Not enjoyment and not sorrow
  Is our destined end or way,

44

But to act, that each tomorrow
  Find us coarser than today.

Art is long and time is fleeting,
  And no matter how we look
Still our secret sins are beating
  Records for a beastlier book.

For the publishers wide battle,
  For this barbecue of "Lives";
Be not like clean peaceful cattle,
  Be a Bluebeard rich in wives.

Trust the future's tales unpleasant,
  Let no past respect its dead
Act, act, in the living present
  For biographers ahead.

Lives of great men all remind us
  We can make our lives unclean,
And, departing, leave behind us
  Data for more books obscene

Stories that perhaps another,
  Tired of misbehavior vain,
A blasé and wearied brother,
  Reading, may begin again.

Let us then be up and doing,
  With a heart for any shame,
Still achieving, still pursuing,
  Learn to live for long ill-fame.

THE WAR-SKUNK

In Spanish wars with Mexico
  The warhorse was an aid
And in old battles of the East
The fighting elephant—dread beast
  Made fleeing foes afraid.

Our battlefield's the newspaper—
    Our weapon is the pen—
And for an ally in the fight
We hire the skunk! our foes take flight!
    Great is the guile of men.

HYENAS

Some write from press of power. So born, they must.
Some write to teach, to spread in widening wave
The cumulative long-sought light of truth.
Some write in patient industry, to earn
Their bread, spread news, teach, please and entertain.
The market changes, and the current taste.
Today, with our Freud-poisoned, sated minds
We grovel like hot guests at Nero's Board,
We weary of the plain primeval lusts,
And must exploit disease, degeneracy,
All foul, bizarre and morbid manias.
Once stories of great men stood up like lamps
To light the path of youth, but we today,
Restricted in attacks on living men,
Dig up the helpless dead to vilify.

Hyenas, those who fail to hunt and kill,
Prowl among graves and drag the corpses out.
Great names are chosen, the long-honored dead,
For on the measure of their fame alone
Rests the cash value of degrading them.
Bones of a thousand years, however great,
Have not the flavor for our present taste.
We want fresh corpses, recognizable,
Still honored and beloved by living men,
That our delight in shaming the great dead
May be enhanced by pain of those alive.
"The truth" they say. True, Cromwell had a wen.

THE YELLOW REPORTER

"Liar!" "You lie!" The word is said—
The blow—the challenge—one lies dead.

This is the answer from rage and shame
To him who has used the blackening name
            of Liar.

"Coward!" Again the deadly blow;
The instant fury that seeks to show
How hotly men resent the shame
Of bearing the unforgivable name
            of Coward.

"Telltale!" Even the child at school,
Though he may be a bully, he may be a fool;
He may cheat—yet he stops at this open shame
He has no friends who hears the name—
            of Telltale.

Spy! though it be his land to save,
Though he be honest and clean and brave,
He must be hanged in helpless shame
If caught at the work that warrants the name
            of Spy.

Yet they today of the Yellow Press
Grow rich in hardened wantonness
By the "nose for news" and the "enterprise"
Of insolent shameless hireling spies—
            Spies!

On sin and sorrow the ferret thrives;
They finger their fellows' private lives,
And noisily publish far and wide
What things their fellows most fair would hide—
            Telltales!

Under the Press Power great and wide
Their unsigned slanders cower and hide
From outraged Justice they slink behind
Shadowy Companies false and blind—
            Cowards!

Guard of Liberty! Guide of Youth!
The Power of the Press is Public truth!
But the Yellow Press—that men may buy—

47

They lie—and lie—and again they lie!
        Liars!

Liar! Coward! Telltale! Spy!
Shame to sell and shame to buy!
Is a wood pulp sheet enough to hide
Who has spied and tattled and skulked and lied?

I Would Fain Die a Dry Death

The American public is patient,
    The American public is slow,
The American public will stand as much
    As any public I know.
We submit to be killed by our railroads,
    We submit to be fooled by our press,
We can stand as much government scandal
    As any folks going, I guess,
We can bear bad air in the subway,
    We can bear quick death in the street,
But we are a little particular
    About the things we eat.

It is not so much that it kills us—
    We are used to being killed;
But we like to know what fills us
    When we pay for being filled.
When we pay the Beef Trust prices,
    As we must, or go without,
It is not that we grudge the money
    But we grudge the horrid doubt.
Is it ham or trichinosis?
    Can a label command belief?
Is it pork we have purchased, or poison?
    Is it tuberculosis or beef?

There is really a choice of diseases,
    To any one, little or big;
And no man really pleases
    To die of a long dead pig.
We take our risks as we're able,

On elevator and train,
But to sit in peace at the table
  And be seized with sudden pain
When we are at home and happy—
  Is really against the grain.

And besides, admitting the poison,
  Admitting we all must die,
Accepting the second-hand sickness
  From a cholera-smitten stye;
Patiently bearing the murder,
  Amiable, meek, inert,—
We do rise up and remonstrate
  Against the Packingtown dirt.
Let there be death in the dinner,
  Subtle and unforeseen,
But O, Mr. Packer, in packing our death,
  Won't you please to pack it clean!

HOW ABOUT THE MAN?

We have seen the picture of Packingtown
Painted in blood-red, black and brown
  As only Sinclair[1] can;
We have heard the story long and sweet
Of how they prepare the food we eat,
We are hearing a plenty about the meat—
  But how about the man?

Somebody did it. Somebody knew—
Somebody excellent profits drew
  From this public poisoning plan;
They are pushing a Bill to finish the fun,—
But think of the mischief that has been done!—
Is there no blame coming to any one?
  How about the man?

He has killed out competitors honest but small,
He's grown rich on the money that comes from us all
  For his death-dealing package and can;
We pay him for meat, but he finds pleasant ways

To feed us on filth, to shorten our days
With ptomaines—and also the prices to raise—
    Now how about the man?

The Packer's Hand

Behold Mr. Packer of Packingtown
    A person of wealth and leisure,
He is well taught and better dressed
And looks like a gentleman like the rest
    As he travels for health and pleasure.

Suppose you meet him—he offers his hand
    As clean as fine soap can make it,
Offers it affably, understand—
With profit and honor at his command;
    But consider, before you take it!

Look at the hand and remember the deeds
    It performs as the Packer pleases,
Set to serve great public needs
And poisoning us for his private greeds
    With chemicals, dirt and diseases;

A skilful hand to escape the law,
    A strong hand able to break it;
So cruel a hand as you ever saw,
Filling the poor blind public maw
With tuberculosis and lumpy jaw,
Trichina and ptomaines, a carrion claw!
    Would you really be willing to shake it!

To the Packer

Here is a man who chooses for his trade
    To feed the public—to provide their meat,
    From the hoofed victim to the package neat,
For which self-chosen task the man is paid.

50

Enormous is his power, and undismayed
  He uses it a million mouths to cheat
  Defiling hideously the food they eat
Distributing diseases trimmed and weighed.
  We buy tuberculosis by the pound
Live parasites and carrion he sells
Poisoning the public as men poison wells;
  Spreading slow death to which no clue is found.
His hands with gold uncounted we have filled
While he, safe, secret, subtle, killed and killed.

A DIET UNDESIRED

He was set to keep a flock of sheep,
And they seemed to him too slow;
So he took great pains to improve their brains
With food to make them grow.

But they would not eat the high-spiced meat
For all that he could say;
His scorn was wasted and the food untasted
For the sheep weren't made that way.

He would make them take his good beefsteak!
So he raged day after day;
But his anger deep was lost on the sheep—
For they were not made that way.

WE EAT AT HOME

We eat at home. We do not care
Of what insanitary fare;
  So that our mother makes the pie
  Content we live, content we die,
And proudly our dyspepsia bear.

Straight from our furred forefather's lair
The instinct comes of feeding there;

51

And still unmoved by progress high
    We eat at home.

In wasteful ignorance we buy
Alone, alone our food we fry—
    What if a tenfold cost we bear?
    The doctor's bill—the dentist's chair?
    Still without ever asking why
        We eat at home.

SPECIAL DRY TOAST
(RAILROAD "DINER")

"Special dry toast"—at fifteen cents;
Once five, then ten, but late events
    Show heights in railroad bills of fare
    At which poor passengers may stare,
Leaving to reckless opulence
    "Special dry toast."

Nor are these portions so immense
As to condone their rank offense;
    Fractions of slices close they pare,
    Three tiny fragments crisping there—
        "Special dry toast."

The public, patient, meek and dense,
Complains not, in its innocence,
    That five-cent loaves, in this wise care,
    Sell for a dollar, share by share,
Well named, in their cool impudence—
    "Special Dry Toast."

THE MELTING POT

A melting pot has to be made
    With particular care,
And carefully sampled and weighed

As to nature, proportion and grade
  Are the ores mingled there.

Let the metaphor change in your mind
  To an effort to bake,
Of eggs, butter, and flour you will find,
With milk, sugar and raisins combined,
  You compose a good cake.

Or, taking salt pepper and meat,
  With an onion or two,
Tomatoes, and maybe a beet,
Fine herbs and some celery sweet,
  A good soup you may brew.

But if all these ingredients here
  Should comingle at will,
Neither cake nor yet soup will appear,
There's one name for a mixture so queer—
  That is swill.

WHY?

To the United States of America
1915—1916

Why does America sit so still,
  Watching all Europe die?
Doing nothing, or good, or ill,
To stop Red Death and Idiot Waste,
While the little nations, closer placed,
Beg for aid of the power we hold?
Why do we sit, unmoved and cold,
  And the need of the world deny?
    Answer, America!—Why?

Why does America stain her hands
  With blood that will never dry?
With war-priced wealth from helpless lands—
Speculating in Death Preferred;
Refusing to let her voice be heard

In the Council of Nations which may avail
To end the Horror? And, though it fail,
  Why should we fail to try?
    Answer, America!—Why?

Why does America turn away
  From Europe's bitter cry?—
Death of the young men day by day,
Ruin of woman and child and land—
War will stop when the nations stand
Leagued together in Union wide;
Why does our nation turn aside
  And let the First Call go by?
    Answer, America!—Why?

ON GERMANY

At last they had the ruffian downed
And his spent captors stood around,
Bleeding and torn in every limb,
To think what they should do with him;
What punishment, and for what time,
Could expiate his hideous crime;
What fine, how long enforced and paid,
Could mend the ruin he had made;
And some who called him maniac sure,
Sought how to best restrain and cure.

But others who had held it wrong
To struggle with the villain strong;
Claiming that it was *never* right,
No matter what the cause, to fight;
Plead with the judges, lest their dealings
Might somehow hurt the prisoners' feelings.

They said, "More honor must be lent
To this so brave belligerent."
"If you should make too sore your sentence
It might postpone his true repentance."
"If you inflict too heavy pain
He may be led to strike again."

54

"If you, by fines, your wealth regained,
His life and children would be pained,
Surely, Oh surely you would scorn
So to impoverish the unborn!"

The victors might have answered thus:
"He's no belligerent, this cuss,
But a plain criminal in fact,
And caught redhanded in the act.
He strike again if we do more?
Without offense he struck before,
And doubtless so will strike again
If we let any chance remain.
And for his feelings—Holy Powers!
Suppose you give a thought to ours.
As to his family—'tis true,
But we have wives and children too,
By him impoverished. Please explain
Why his alone should not have pain?
All the unborn the loss must bear,
We propose his shall have their share."

They might have answered thus, or longer,
They have answered even stronger?
They might, but it seemed too protracted,
The court was sitting, and it acted.

THE INTERNATIONALIST

He spoke with pride as a superior soul,
    "I am an Internationalist" said he,
No pent up Utica of native land
Commands allegience of my heart & hand,
I am not thrilled by any flag unfurled
Unless it be the flag of all the world,
    Nationless, free."

"An Internationalist," I slow replied,
    "Nation" I know, and "inter" is between,
But in between the nations, on the map,
There is no room for anyone, poor chap!

55

Their borders touch—still, if you so hate slaughter,
You might be International—in water,
    At sea, I mean.

When nations as our states have done, unite
    Each seeing the advantage due to him,
A Federated World will surely grow,
By natural laws which we already know,
But if no native land you can endure,
And this adopted one you find so poor—
    Go swim! Go swim!

WE AND HONDURAS

Forty-three nations have joined the League,
    Over the world so wide—
But we—and little Honduras—
    We stay outside!

Seven were not invited,
    Five of our world-war foes—
And two that are somewhat unsettled—
    We stand with those!

We ought to be proud of our company
    As history proves our pride—
Forty-three nations that joined the League
    Nine left outside.

Seven left out on judgement
    For incompetence or crime—
And the two who were asked, and wouldn't join—
    Stand for all time.

Famous indeed the record
    As History will decide,
To work to serve the world
    Forty-three nations decide—
But We—and little Honduras
    We stood outside.

An Army With Banners

Together men faced the mammoth,
   Together men stood to fight,
Together knew life and glory,
   Together met death and night.
And because they stood together,
   For the safety of the whole,
Courage and comradeship were born—
   The ancient army's soul.

While, all the years, poor, weak, dull-eyed, alone,
The men who toiled, toiled on, each for his own.

   The army was rich with banners,
      The uniforms gay with gold.
   To music the charge rushed headlong,
      To music their steps were told.
   They were strong in their conscious numbers,
      They were led by a clear command,
   And the glory of each was glory
      Because all could understand.

Bannerless, silent, in ignoble dress,
Men toiled, alone, in dim confused distress.

   Yet the deeds of the army with banners
      Were of slaughter and pain and strife,
   While the deeds of the bannerless lonely men
      Keep all the world in life.
   Some day they will see that their work is one,
      In the service of the whole—
   Then the standards rise and the music cries,
      And the army finds its soul.

Pikers

"Sit in! Sit in!" cry the Nations,
  "Sit in to the greatest game
    That ever was played

Since man was made
For Progress & Peace and Fame!"

"We play against War and Famine,
    Pestilence, Ruin and Shame—
        We stake our best
        With all the rest—
Sit in! And play the game!

Great and small came the nations
    Over the earth's expanse
        Small and great
        Piled state on state
To play for the world's advance.

But one—God pity the pikers!
    One was afraid to play!
        We might lose, they said,
        If we went ahead,
We might have to fight—or pay!

Forty-three others are willing,
    Forty-three others share,
        For the common need
        They forget their greed,
But we—God pity the pikers!—we do not dare!

WOMEN OF 1920

On the Women of 1920
    So newly freed—
Hangs the fate of a nation—
The pride or shame of a nation—
    God guide their deed!

Will the women of 1920
    Drink party hate
Sink to the grade of a party—
Believe the cant of a party—
Forget the world for a party
    And repent—too late?

58

Will the women of 1920
  Hear the world's appeal?
Forty three nations together
Ask us to join together
With them and stand together
  For the common weal.

On the women of 1920
  The choice must fall.
Shall we join in with the others
Dare and bear with the others
Or stand apart from the others
  Shamed before all?

O Women of 1920
  This is your home!
On you hangs your country's honor—
World safety, Peace and honor
You have the choice and the home
  You have the power!

More Females of the Species
(After Kipling)

When the traveller in the pasture meets the he-bull in his pride,
He shouts to scare the monster, who will often turn aside;
But the milch cow, thus accosted, pins the traveller to the rail—
For the female of the species is deadlier than the male.

When Nag, the raging stallion, meets a careless man on foot,
He will sometimes not destroy him, even if the man don't shoot;
But the mare, if he should meet one, makes the bravest cowboy
    pale—
For the female of the species is more deadly than the male.

When our first colonial settlers met the Hurons and Choctaws,
They were burned and scalped and slaughtered by the fury-
    breathing squaws;
'Twas the women, not the warriors, who in war-paint took the
    trail—
For the female of the species is more deadly than the male.

59

Man's timid heart is bursting with the things he must not say
As to women, lest in speaking he should give himself away;
But when he meets a woman—see him tremble and turn pale—
For the female of the species is more deadly than the male.

Lay your money on the hen-fight! On the dog-fight fought by shes!
On the gory Ladies Prize-fight—there are none so fierce as these!
See small girls each other pounding, while their peaceful brothers
    wail—
For the female of the species is more deadly than the male.

So in history they tell us how all China shrieked and ran
Before the wholesale slaughter dealt by Mrs. Genghis Khan.
And Attila, the Scourge of God, who made all Europe quail,
Was a female of the species and more deadly than the male.

Red war with all its million dead is due to female rage,
The names of women murderers monopolize the page,
The pranks of a Napoleon are nothing to the tale
Of destruction wrought by females, far more deadly than the male.

In the baleful female infant this ferocity we spy,
It glares in bloodshot fury from the maiden's dewy eye,
But the really deadly female, when you see her at her best,
Has two babies at her petticoat and a suckling at her breast.

Yet hold! there is Another! A monster even worse!
The Terror of Humanity! Creation's direst curse!
Before whom men in thousands must tremble, shrink and fail—
A sanguinary Grandma—more deadly than the male!

THE GUNMAN

Prowling in the alley, loafing in the bar,
Chancing his swift "get-away" in a stolen car;
Vermin of the city, whose bite is sure to kill,
Hired by wiser villains to work vicarious ill;
Not for hate or vengeance or quarrel of his own,
In sordid risk and danger this savage strikes alone.
Life to him is merchandise, crime he sneers away,

Carelessly he murders for a little pay,
Killing, for his profit, a man he never saw—
Thug—assassin—gunman—laughing at the law.
Honored and defended by church and bench and bar,
Proud in his park and palace, steam yacht and private car,
Giver to school and college, to charitable care,
Patron of art and science, a multi-millionaire.
He makes the guns and sells them; again and yet again
There die, to his advantage, our armies of young men.
Not for hate or vengeance, or quarrel of his own
He kills, but just for business, for profit his alone.
Murderer of millions, by him our wars are made;
Thug—assassin—gunman—thriving at his trade.

THE POWDERED NOSE

The powder over her nose
  Shines like a looming lighthouse,
Far in the distance shows the powder
The powder over her nose.
Whiter than winter's snows,
  Whiter far than the White House,
The powder over her nose
Shines like a looming lighthouse.

———————

"Why do you powder your nose"? I asked,
  "Death white in a painted face,"
She answered gravely, "You don't suppose
That I'd be seen with a shiny nose
  In a public place!"

"Though as large" said I "as a nose can be,
  "And greasy, there still is hope,
The whitewash blazons it far and wide,
And proves the grease that you wish to hide—
  Why not try soap?"

A SOCIAL PUZZLE

Society sat musing, very sad,
Upon her people's conduct, which was bad.

Said she, "I can't imagine why they sin,
With all the education I put in!
For instance, why so many maimed and sick
After their schooling in arithmetic?
Why should they cheat each other beyond telling
When they were so well grounded in good spelling?
They learned geography by land and tribe,
And yet my statesmen can't refuse a bribe!
Ought not a thorough knowledge of old Greek
To lead to that wide peace the nations seek?
And grammar! With their grammar understood
Why should they still shed one another's blood?
Then, lest these ounces of prevention fail,
I've pounds and tons of cure—of no avail.
I punish terribly, and I have cause,
When they so sin against my righteous laws."

"Of grammar?" I enquired. She look perplexed.
"For errors in their spelling?" She grew vexed.
"Failure in mathematics?" "You young fool!"
She said, "The law don't meddle with the school.
I teach with care and cost, but never ask
What conduct follows from the early task.
My punishment, for all the law's wide reach,
Is in the lines I don't pretend to teach."

I meditated. Does one plant him corn—
Then weep because no oranges are born?

High Sovereignty

I like to see my little dog
    Hop round me on the floor,
Unnaturally vertical
    As dogs were not before.

It is no earthly use to him,—
    No earthly use to me,—
But I delight in it because
    It proves my sovereignty.

I like to seem him hold a lump
   Of sugar on his paw,
And never dare to eat it up
   Till I lay down the law.

I watch his slow disjointed meals
   With pleasure most refined—
It shows how powerful I am
   To make the creature mind.

God made him on four legs to run,
   No doubt with purpose good;
But I can make him hop on two,
   And go without his food!

This Is a Lady's Hat
(A Trio of Triolets.)

This is a lady's hat—
   To cover the seat of reason;
It may look like a rabbit or bat,
Yet this is a lady's hat;
May be ugly, ridiculous, that
   We never remark, 'twould be treason.
This is a lady's hat,
   To cover the seat of reason.

* * *

These are a lady's shoes,
   Ornaments, curved and bended,
But feet are given to use,
Not merely to show off shoes,
To stand, walk, run if we choose,
   For which these were never intended.
These are a lady's shoes.
   Ornaments, curved and bended.

* * *

This is a lady's skirt,
   Which limits her locomotion;

63

Her shape is so smooth-begirt
As to occupy all the skirt,
Of being swift and alert
    She has not the slightest notion;
This is a lady's skirt,
    Which limits her locomotion.

BIG HATS—WOMEN'S—AT BASE BALL!

When we pay good cash for our places
And carefully choose the same—
We want to watch the balls and bats—
We don't want to look at your hats!
We don't want to look at your faces!
We want to look at the game!

HER HAT STILL WITH US

So big, so black—so shapeless, so oppressive,
So heavy, overhanging and excessive,
Huge shadowy, bulk—a bier? a bush? no, worse
A cross between a haystack and a hearse.

MRS. NOAH

These ladies so slender and stark,
Whose garments surround them like bark,
    May be fair in the face,
    But for outline and grace
They are like Mrs. Noah of the ark.

THE CRIPPLE

There are such things as feet, human feet,
But these she does not use;

64

Firm and supple, white and sweet,
Softly graceful, lightly fleet,
For comfort, beauty, service meet—
These are feet, human feet,
These she doth with scorn refuse—
Preferring shoes.

There are such things as shoes, human shoes,
Though scant and rare the proof;
Serviceable, soft and strong,
Pleasant, comely, wearing long,
Easy as a well known song—
These are shoes, human shoes,
But from these she holds aloof—
Prefers the hoof!

There are such things as hoofs, sub-human hoofs,
High-heeled sharp anomalies;
Small and pinching, hard and black,
Shiny as a beetle's back,
Cloven, clattering on the track,
These are hoofs, sub-human hoofs,
She cares not for truth, nor ease—
Preferring these!

A PROTEST

O mother! mother! cried the babe,
   Why must I lie so warm?
With woolens thick
That clog and stick
   All round my feeble form?

I want to stretch and feel myself
   I want to wiggle there—
Why don't you pull
This heap of wool?
   Why don't you warm the air?

O mother! cried the little maid,
   Why must my dress be fine?

While brother goes
In knicks and hose,
  Why are these ruffles mine?

I want to run and roll and climb,
  To play, perhaps to fight!
He tumbles down,
Unblamed, in brown—
  Why must I mince in white?

His cap is easy on his head,
  Alert and free his face—
Why must I wear
O'er eyes and hair
  This cauliflower of lace?

Why trail these yards of lengthening skirt
  By his brief trouser line?
If I'm so weak
O mother, speak!
  Why must the weight be mine?

The mother answered never a word,
  But from her eyes shone through
The primal pride
Of the savage bride
  In a veil of rich tattoo.

No mercy had she on herself,
  No mercy on the child;
As gods to her
Are plume and fur,
  By beads is she beguiled.

THE SPEAKER'S SIN

It was a lovely lady
With manners of the best;
She was finely educated

66

She was exquisitely dressed.
With a topic philanthropic
She arose to fill her place
In the program which was builded
For to elevate the race.
She arose with highest purpose
Her noble best to do—
There were seven other ladies
Who were on the program too.

The lady read her paper
Till her hearers wore a frown;
The chairman was a lady
And she would not ring her down;
And when the chairman hinted
That her limit long was o'er
The lady with the paper
Asked for just a minute more!
The hearers were all ladies,
What could the hearers do?
There were seven other ladies
Upon the program too!

And those seven other ladies
Had to summon grace sublime
To smile and wait in silent state
While the speaker stole their time.

Eight speakers in a two hour space
Gives each a fair amount,
Could not the lady read the score
Of those who also claimed the floor?
Could not the lady count?
Did she imagine that her theme
Was the only subject there?
Or that her treatment was the best
And no one wished to hear the rest?
Was it that she forgot their feeling
Who had to lose what she was stealing?
Or that she did not care?

AGE AND "YOUTH"
("CRABBED YOUTH AND AGE CANNOT LIVE TOGETHER.")

No ground for putting on airs, old friend,
    Counting years you have wiggled through,
There's many a pauper and villain and fool
Bird in the tree and fish in the pool
    As old, or older than you.

Not dying proves little when all is said,
    As the poets have seen and sung,
Those by whom all the world was led
Were often survived by the "better dead"—
    "Whom the gods love die young."

No ground for putting on airs, young friend,
    Because you are young and new,
There's many a donkey beside its dam,
Cotton-tail rabbit and wooly lamb
    As young and younger than you.

The Hope of the World is in Youth, you say,
    Verdant her robe is seen;
But we may look back for a very long way,
Where each generation was young in its day,
    And still see something green.

Our wounds are not to be helped by age,
    And not to be healed by youth,
What the world needs to dry its tears
Is no poor pride about days and years
    But Wisdom and Courage and Truth.

THE LOVE OF HUMAN KIND

O fast we hold to those we love
    And clutch them to our hearts
But still the soul desires the whole—
    And what are these but parts?

O fast we hold to those we love
    As we would drink them dry—
But still our hearts are not sufficed
    And still for hunger cry—

Sweet is the love of man and maid—
    The mother for the child
But there's a love more tender far;
    More passionate and wild.

Close is the love of one for one
    But there is larger worth
In the dear love of human kind
    All over the green earth.

We need not lose the little love—
    So easy, old, and dear
But we must find the larger kind
    That holds all others here.

THE BITTEN GRASS

The bitten grass! The close-mown grass!
    The poor earth bare and dry
Then pastures green and cornfields sheen
    As all the years go by.

For still the grass, the blessed grass,
    Knows neither death nor dearth,
Thick sweet and fine, in shade and shine
    All over the green earth.

We need not grieve mown fields to leave
    Nor close cropped pastures bare—
Though grassblades go in utter wo—
    The grass! The grass is there!

The slaughtered men! the driven men!
    The poor oppressed race!
The blood and tears of endless years—
    What can such grief efface!

No creature born so worked and worn
    No tale so sad to tell—
No lives one sees increase like these—
    No creature thrives so well!

In every land how thick they stand
    Ever more strong, more dear—
The swift years show how strong they grow
    Mankind! Mankind! is here.

ANOTHER CREED

Another creed! We're all so pleased!
A gentle tentative new creed. We're eased
Of all those things we couldn't quite believe
But would not give the lie to. Now perceive
How charmingly this suits us! Science even
Has naught against our modern views of Heaven;
And yet the most emotional of women
May find this creed a warm deep sea to swim in.

Here's something now so loose and large of fit
That all the churches may come under it,
And we may see upon the earth once more
A church united—as we had before!
Before so much of precious blood was poured
That each in his own way might serve the Lord.
All wide divergence in sweet union sunk—
Like branches growing up into a trunk!

And in our intellectual delight
In this sweet formula that sets us right;
And controversial exercises gay
With those who still prefer a differing way;
And our glad effort to make known this wonder
And get all others to unite thereunder—
We, joying in this newest, best of creeds,
Continue still to do our usual deeds!

The Queen

They laid before her conquering feet
    The spoils of many lands,
Their crowns shone red upon her head
    Their scepters in her hands.

* * *

She heard two murmuring at night
    Where rose-sweet shadows rest,
And coveted the blossom red
    He laid upon her breast.

The Fool Killer

O Executioner long sought on every side!
Thou hast arrived at length
And mowest down the proud fool in his pride
The strong fool in his strength.

The weak fool in his weakness so immense,
The old fool in his age,
The young fool in his downy innocence—
The pen-fool in his page.

We knew not Justice even now had found us
In wisdom wide—
The fool is dying everywhere around us—
By suicide.

He dieth by slow poison—he will eat it!
No man may save him nay;
He seeketh death and goeth out to meet it—
O Death—meet him half way!

Kitchen Women

A shallow creature, empty-minded, weak:
Given to foolish pleasures like a child;

Eager for presents, not ashamed to ask;
Glad of each holiday and idle hour;
And flirting with a shy self-interest
With the young master—that may chance to be:—
But what can you expect of kitchen maids?

Sordid and narrow! valuing a man
By what he brings to her of clothes and food;
By his ability to pay the bills,
And willingness to listen to her talk
Of the small interests in a narrow life;
His patience with her failures, and his praise
Of her crude labors and attempts to please.
No knowledge of his business, and no help
In troubles and temptations of his work:—
But what can you expect of kitchen wives?

Anxious and weary, fretful, overstrained,
Telling the clinging child to "Go away—
Mother is busy!" Busy all the time,
With labors that leave nothing for the child
Of a glad mother's rich companionship,
Of a wise mother's well-adjusted care,
Of a strong mother's ever-ready help:—
How can these come of kitchen motherhood?

Then, being freed of labor for themselves
Beggars on horseback, merciless and proud,
How harsh they are to women they command,
(Servants of servants—masters always hard!)
How savagely they decorate themselves
With skins and feathers and all shining stones,
And hang their houses with crude ornament,
The flaunting foliage of a fruitless tree—
Senseless expression of a soul unused
To speak through channels worthy of mankind!

Still superstitious and conservative,
Prejudiced, timid, cruel as the grave
To those who sin against their little creed;
Swayed easily by every passing breath
Of fashion, with no thought to govern it;
And still their utmost wish to lavish all

The labor they can buy upon the House,
Table, and Body they have served so long.

Unhappy world, that struggles to be great
Be wise, be true, be daring and be free!
These kitchen-minded women keep it back.

THE HOUSEWIFE

Here is the House to hold me—cradle of all the race;
Here is my lord and my love, here are my children dear—
Here is the House enclosing, the dear-loved dwelling place;
Why should I ever weary for aught that I find not here?

Here for the hours of the day and the hours of the night;
Bound with the bands of Duty, rivetted tight;
Duty older than Adam—Duty that saw
Acceptance utter and hopeless in the eyes of the serving squaw.

Food and the serving of food—that is my daylong care;
What and when we shall eat, what and how we shall wear;
Soiling and cleaning of things—that is my task in the main—
Soil them and clean them and soil them—soil them and clean them
    again.

To work at my trade by the dozen and never a trade to know;
To plan like a Chinese puzzle—fitting and changing so;
To think of a thousand details, each in a thousand ways;
For my own immediate people and a possible love and praise.

My mind is trodden in circles, tiresome, narrow and hard,
Useful, commonplace, private—simply a small back-yard;
And I the Mother of Nations!—Blind their struggle and vain!—
I cover the earth with my children—each with a housewife's brain.

THE PROPOSAL

To be a wife! . . . . He asks of me
Life's love, the heart's long loyalty,

That I join his life to my own
And of all men choose him alone
The father of my child to be.

Beloved—yes! Together we
Can work, can grow, our trades agree.—
    What! You demand domestic Joan?
    And I must toil at your hearthstone
        To be a wife?

Beloved!—listen—can't you see
That wifehood is not cookery?
    That mother's love, that woman's heart
    In kitchen service need no part?
My work is chosen—yet I'm free
    To be a wife.

ODE TO THE COOK

O Cook! Domestic Cook! no exhumed stone
In ancient dignity can match thine own.
Crete or Abydos fail to throw their light
So far adown our pro-social night.
Behind the bronze—behind chipped stone we look—
With first discovered fire we find the cook!
That fire, from hearthstone winning wide its place,
Now world-encircling service gives our race;
But thou alone remainest, all unmoved, alone
Tending thy pots around that primal stone
Where once the squaw made moccasins of hide.
We web the world in fabrics woven wide;
Where toiled she her poor shelter to erect
Now plans the engineer and architect;
Where the lone crone o'er naked babes held rule
Our children know the college and the school;
Art has arisen, science lights and leads;
Labor enriches life with wondrous deeds;
But while the ages urge us, shock on shock,
Thou standest, changeless as primeval rock—
Unchangeable, immovable—we see
Our race's earliest infancy in thee!

74

Deaf patience and blind habit; and the dumb
Submission of long ages—these have come
To thee instead of progress. Must thou last
Forever?—type of Paleolithic past!

The Eternal Mother to the Bachelor Maid

Child! poor child! So little and so weak!
    Lift your head and try to see
    Down the ages back of thee—
      Hear the ages speak!

Life! One life! Since first acknowledged good,
    Links o'erlapping endlessly,
    Embodied immortality—
      That is motherhood!

Life! All Life! Outspreading like a fan;
    But each line going back and back
    Along the smooth, unbroken track
      Where motherhood began.

Life! Our Life! This world of friend and foe—
    Brothers all by ties of blood
    Through our common motherhood
      A million years ago!

Child! Blind child! *We* are the endless dream;
    We, the fountain; we, the source;
    We the guiders of the course
      Of the unbroken stream.

Rise! Now rise! Take your appointed place!
    Wise and strong as ne'er before—
    Human, free, but all the more
      The mother of the race!

Two Callings

I hear a deep voice through uneasy dreaming,
    A deep, soft, tender, soul-beguiling voice;

A lulling voice that bids the dreams remain,
That calms my restlessness and dulls my pain,
That thrills and fills and holds me till in seeming
    There is no other sound on earth—no choice.

"Home!" says the deep voice, "Home!" and softly singing
    Brings me a sense of safety unsurpassed;
So old! So old! The piles above the wave—
The shelter of the stone-blocked shadowy cave—
Security of sun-kissed treetops swinging—
    Safety and Home at last!

"Home" says the sweet voice, and warm Comfort rises,
    Holding my soul with velvet-fingered hands;
Comfort of leafy lair and lapping fur,
Soft couches, cushions, curtains, and the stir
Of easy pleasures that the body prizes,
    Of soft swift feet to serve the least commands.

I shrink—half rise—and then it murmurs "Duty!"
    Again the past rolls out—a scroll unfurled:
Allegiance and long labor due my lord—
Allegiance in an idleness abhorred—
I am the squaw—the slave—the harem beauty—
I serve and serve the handmaid of the world.

My soul revels—but hark! a new note thrilling,
    Deep, deep, past finding—I protest no more;
The voice says "Love!" and all those ages dim
Stand glorified and justified in him,
I bow—I kneel—the woman soul is willing—
    "Love is the law. Be still! Obey! Adore!"

And then—ah then! The deep voice murmurs "Mother!"
    And all life answers from the primal sea;
A mingling of all lullabies, a peace
That asks no understanding; the release
Of nature's holiest power—who seeks another?
    Home? Home is Mother—Mother, Home, to me.

"Home!" says the deep voice; "Home and Easy Pleasure!"
    Safety and Comfort Laws of Life well kept!
"Love!" and my heart rose thrilling at the word;

"Mother!" it nestled down and never stirred;
"Duty and Peace and Love beyond all measure!
    Home! Safety! Comfort! Mother!"—and I slept.

II

A bugle call! A clear keen ringing cry
    Relentless—eloquent—that found the ear
Through fold on fold of slumber, sweet, profound—
A widening wave of universal sound,
Piercing the heart—filling the utmost sky—
    I wake—I must wake! Hear—for I must hear!

"The World! The World is crying! Hear its needs!"
    Home is a part of life—I am the whole!
Home is the cradle—shall a whole life stay
Cradled in comfort through the working day?
I too am Home—the Home of all high deeds—
    The only Home to hold the human soul!

"Courage!—the front of conscious life!" it cried;
    "Courage that dares to die and dares to live!
Why should you prate of safety? Is life meant
In ignominious safety to be spent?
Is Home best valued as a place to hide?—
    Come out, and give what you are here to give!"

"Strength and Endurance! of high action born!"
    And all that dream of Comfort shrank away,
Turning its fond, beguiling face aside—
So Selfishness and Luxury and Pride
Stood forth revealed, till I grew fierce with scorn,
    And burned to meet the dangers of the day.

"Duty! Ah Duty! Duty! Mark the word!"
    I turned to my old standard. It was sent
From hem to hem, and through the gaping place
I saw at last its meaning and its place
I saw my undone duties to the race
Of man—neglected—spurned—how had I heard
    That word and never dreamed of what it meant!

"Duty! Unlimited—eternal—new!"
    And I? My idol on a petty shrine

Fell as I turned, and Cowardice and Sloth
Fell too, unmasked, false Duty covering both—
While the true Duty, all-embracing, high,
   Showed the clear line of noble deed to do.

And then the great voice rang out to the sun,
   And all my terror left me, all my shame,
While every dream of joy from earliest youth
Came back and lived!—that joy unhoped was truth,
All joy, all hope, all truth, all peace grew one,
   Life, opened clear, and Love? Love was its name!

So when the great word "Mother!" rang once more,
   I saw at last its meaning and its place,
Not the blind passion of the brooding past,
But Mother—the World's Mother—came at last,
To love as she had never loved before—
   To feed and guard and teach the human race.

The world was full of music clear and high!
   The world was full of light! The world was free!
And I? Awake at last, in joy untold
Saw Love and Duty broad as life unrolled—
Wide as the earth—unbounded as the sky—
   Home was the World—the World was Home to me!

LIMITING LIFE

   "Life is too numerous!" said he,
   And rushed into the strife,
   With fang and beak and talon red,
   With horn and hoof and butting head,
      To limit life.

   "Life is too numerous," said he,
   And wilder rose the strife;
   With crimson war-clouds rolling dense—
   Vice, poverty and pestilence—
      To limit life.

"Life grows too numerous," saith she
Who is not built for strife;
"Through me it cometh, swift or slow;
I will decide how fast to grow—
To limit life."

THE SANTA CLAUS STORY

The Santa Claus story is funny and gay,
    And pleasant and loving too;
But the Christ-child story is lovlier far,
With the dear God's love for all that are,
As warm as the sun and as bright as the star,
    And the Christ-child story is true!

A VANDAL

"M. Lane. Brewster. New York."
    Deserves some local fame,
For having with malice a forethought
    Deliberately carved his name
On the half-inch-wide
Thin strip at the side
    Of a day-coach window frame.

On the New York Central and Hudson,
    Car seventeen fifty-nine,
You may read, with your head turned sideways,
    That soul-betraying sign,
Fourth right, my friend,
As you face the end
    Where the twin inscriptions shine.

Idle and empty-headed,
    Without book or paper or game,
He saw something smooth and shiny,
    And scarred it with his name;
With a knife or a pin

79

He scratched it in
  On the varnished window frame.

To Poverty

Eyes so long in darkness they may not use their sight!
 Mind content in ignorance and heart inured to ill!
Soul so seared by sorrow it thrills to no delight,
 So overmastered and despoiled it knoweth not its will!
The wine of life untasted, the light of life unknown,
The hopes of life along the way like withered roses strown,
 All unwitting of the joy the sons of men may claim,
 Unmindful of their royal birth and more than royal name,
Content to build the heavy walls that all their lives immure—
Mistress of all mysteries, that poison dwarf and maim,
Poverty hath worked her will and made the people poor!

Art hath clothed and covered her with raiment fair and white,
 Hiding the baleful warning front with many a fold and fill;
Literature hath lied for her, from far Olympic height,
 Drama and song defend her door and guard the flower strewn sill.
Reason behind her walks in chains that ring of power to own
Truth and Liberty lie bound and dumb before the throne
 Fed by the haughty charity of pious lord and dame,
 Nursed by a servile senseless love—a love that has no aim,
Sheltered by a coward Church behind the Master pure—
 Even Science shielding her! All prostrate here the same!
Poverty hath worked her will and made the people poor!

She hunts mankind with all her pack of wants that gnaw and bite,
 The strong man groans beneath her hand and woman waileth shrill,
She snares hot youth and strangles it with clutches cold and tight,
 She hounds the trembling feet of age all helpless, down the hill,
And while our fathers say no word, our mothers make no moan,
And Justice sits, not only blind, but deaf as graven stone,
 Low laughing at the easy range of her defenseless game
She sets her wolves along the path where once the children came
Where little children used to come, in peace and health secure—
 Look on them now! The eyes of age in a child's distorted frame!
Poverty hath worked her will and made the people poor!

Look at her work! The deafened ear, the eye devoid of light,
　The empty mind whose shattered cup no stream of thought can fill,
The crippled limb, the shrunken form, the thing that prowls by night,
　The weary, hopeless grinding pain that only death can still.
By that which cometh out of it her fateful power is shown—
By the poison fruit of the poison tree its deadly name is known—
　By those no honor can arouse, no high desire inflame,
　So used to daily misery, so used to scorn and blame,
They answer not to any call, they heed no sweetest lure—
　Degraded past, redemption—ruined beyond reclaim—
Poverty hath worked her will and made the people poor!

Out of these what good may come? What wish to live aright?
　The joyous hands that made the world with eager power and skill
Stiffened and cramped by sordid tasks or sunk in craven flight,
　They on whose strength our lives depend now minded but to kill—
Our place and progress resting still on these so helpless grown,
We reaping still at these poor hands the fruit that we have sown,
　They whose proud courage makes his safe are crouching weak and
　　tame,
　Whose swift advance should lead the world lagging infirm and
　　lame,
Whose grievous state cries out on us with verdict stern and sure—
　Let these dull wrecks of human life their awful cause proclaim—
Poverty hath worked her will and made the people poor!

Envoy

World where wealth is virtue! World where wealth is fame!
Wealth is made by human hands and human hearts aflame!
　With a race of sunk and sodden men what fortune can endure?
Waken to your danger now! Waken to your shame!
　Poverty hath worked her will and made the people poor!

THE LORD OF STRIFE

Came a time in history—
　The history of Life—
When the male—so long inferior—
Claimed to be the born superior
　As the Lord of Strife.

81

He looked down on industry—
   Work was made for slaves!
Woman's life they made servility—
All the prizes and nobility
   Went to warlike Braves!

Age of death and victory—
   Of blood & tears and pain—
Of war-lords age of warriors—
While the farmer, weaver, quarrier,
   Were ruled and robbed and slain!

Nations rose to majesty
   Through labor—wise and slow,
Then came warlike masculinity—
Homicidal assininity—
   Laid the nations low.

Oft-repeated tragedy!
   Yet no tongue or pen
Showed the check to real humanity
In the monstrous baseless vanity
   Of these fighting men.

RELIGIOUS TOLERATION

A loud long cry is pouring forth,
   East and west and south and north,
Demanding of our patient nation
   More religious toleration.

What tiny sect for safety cries?
   Under what sudden consternation?
Against what persecution rise
   These pleaders for our toleration?

The largest of all churches there
   Among our varied population,
And one not noted anywhere
   For its religious toleration.

In every country, period, race,
    Their record stands for contemplation,
Faith, Hope, and Charity have place—
    But not religious toleration.

Should that great power be raised again,
    And dominate our once free nation,
Then might we beg, and beg in vain,
    For our religious toleration.

THE REAL RELIGION

Man, the hunter, Man, the warrior;
Slew for gain and slew for safety,
Slew for rage, for sport, for glory—
    Slaughter was his breath:
So the man's mind, searching inward,
Saw in all one red reflection,
Filled the world with dark religions
    Built on Death.

Death and The Fate of The Soul;—
The soul, from the body dissevered;
Through the withering failure of age,
Through the horror and pain of disease,
Through raw wounds and destruction and fear:—
In fear, black fear of the dark,
Red fear of terrible gods,
Sent forth on its journey, alone,
To eternity, fearful, unknown—
Death, and The Fate of the Soul.

———————

Woman, bearer; Woman, teacher;
Overflowing love and labor,
Service of the tireless mother
    Filling all the earth;—
Now her mind, awakening, searching,
Sees a fair world, young and growing,
Sees at last our real religion—
    Built on Birth.

83

Birth, and The Growth of The Soul;—
The Soul, in the body established;
In the ever-new beauty of childhood,
In the wonder of opening power,
Still learning, improving, achieving;
In hope, new knowledge and light,
Sure faith in the world's fresh Spring,—
Together we live, we grow,
On the earth that we love and know—
Birth, and the Growth of the Soul.

Part Two
The Philosopher

A Central Sun

Given a central sun—and a rolling world;
  Into the light we whirl—and call it day;
  Into the dark we turn—and call it night;
Glow of the dawn—glory of mid-day light—
Shadow of eve—rest of the flower-sweet night—
  And the dawn again!

Given a constant Soul—and a passing form;
  Into the light we grow—and call it life;
  Into the dark we go—and call it death;
Glory of youth—beauty and pride and power—
Shadow of age—rest of the final hour—
  And are born again!

Patient Truth

Truth sat around, undated,
  A million years ago;
Sat and yawned and waited
To be appreciated;
Offered the facts and waited,
  Waited for us to know.

But we filled our minds with tradition
  From the days of our savage youth;
We worshipped in superstition,
And murdered the brain's ambition
That questioned our superstition—
  What did we care for Truth?

And still we sit here contented,
  Sure that the first is last;
So far as it can be prevented
We oppose the unprecedented,

All progress that can be prevented
　　We prevent, preferring the past.

But Truth is not in a hurry,
　　Truth does not seem to care.
She does not grieve nor worry
At our dullness sloth or flurry,
She does not have to worry—
　　Just keeps on being there.

The Rabbit, The Rhinoceros & I

The Spirit of Philosophy descended
　　In a manner metaphysical and free,
Her Aegis she impartially extended
　　On the Rabbit, the Rhinoceros and me.
　　　　And I stopped upon my Walk
　　　　To hear the Rabbit talk,
　　And the elderly Rhinoceros agree.

The Rabbit was coherently upbraiding
　　The fate that made his soft and tender frame;
And the foes that were eternally invading
　　The furry guards and borders of the same.
　　　　"If my leap was ten times longer—
　　　　If my teeth were ten times stronger—"
　　Said he thought he'd turn the tables in the game.

His companion heard these mournful lucubrations,
　　And remarked that he was practical and old;
"It's a pity that we all have limitations,
　　But it doesn't do us any good to scold.
　　　　Our shape and size are given
　　　　By conditions that we live in,
　　As the shape and size of jelly in a mould.

"Evolutionary forces have assisted
　　In more years than a Rhinoceros can tell
To make my hide so horrid thick and twisted—
　　To give you fur—and enemies, as well.
　　　　What life we have was made

In past ages, I'm afraid—
We can only grin and bear it for a spell."

"May I join your causerie?" I asked politely,
"May I add my jeremiad to the tale?"
I then discoursed on Human Nature tritely,
In a melancholy, modulated wail.
Said "This world's a vale of tears,
And man's little space of years
Can only add more tears to fill the vale."

They turned upon me then in wrath outrageous,
"The fault is yours," they cried, "if you are sad!"
We can not choose surroundings advantageous;
We suffer helpless, helpless we are glad.
Environment to us is fate—
But you can always change the slate,
And make the things that make you good and bad."

The Spirit of Philosophy departed;
The Rabbit and Rhinoceros were dumb.
But I became a little lighter hearted,
I saw a heaven in sight and wanted some.
If our conditions make us sad—
And new conditions may be had—
What hinders us from making Kingdom Come?

THE OYSTER & THE STARFISH

Sat a fat & juicy oyster in a large & lumpy shell,
Came a sucker-fingered starfish who digested oysters well.

When the oyster comprehended that the Starfish was on hand
He contracted his one muscle, like the strongest rubber band.

Slow the Starfish spread his fingers sitting on the Oyster's back,
Found the shell quite hard & solid, couldn't feel the smallest crack.

So he set his suckers sucking, in no haste & with no doubt;
Sat and sucked and pulled and waited for the Oyster to give out.

Time will weary any muscle, and the suckers, rows and rows,
Pulled the shell a little open, made a crack he could not close.

Though the Starfish could not really make the Oyster open wide,
Through the crack he poked his stomach, and digested him
    inside.

Safe from all external dangers yet the oyster surely died,
While that soft extruded stomach ate him in his own inside.

But that Oyster, food for Starfish, did no suicidal sin,
Did not try to Oysterize him! did not ask him to come in!

THE FATALIST AND THE SAILORMAN

Said the Fatalist to the Sailorman
   "Vain are your efforts, vain,
    To cross the windswept main,
For the wind blows where it listeth
And drives you forward and back,
You are but a chip that twisteth
Among currents strong and black.
   The wind is the breath of Fate—
   Lie in your berth and wait."

Said the Sailorman to the Fatalist
   "You're right about the wind,
    But why should I stay behind?
The wind blows where it listeth
To drive me forward or back,
But the art of sailing consisteth
Largely in learning to tack.
   Why should I loaf and wait?
   I know how to tack, on Fate!"

THE WEEPING NAUTILUS

I.

Upon a broad and placid beach,
   Beside the billows' swell,

I mused upon the human race
  Which doeth all things well;
When I heard a chambered nautilus
  A-weeping in his shell.

II.

In fair boat of radiant pearl,
  With silver sail and oar,
On sunlit waves we floated there,
  A little way from shore;
And yet that chambered nautilus
  Did sob and sorrow sore.

III.

My heart went out in sympathy
  Across the shallow sea;
Thought I, "with form so beautiful
  And life so fair and free,
A thing to make this creature weep
  An awful thing must be!"

IV.

So I asked him most respectfully,
  With interest sincere.
If he would tell me why he wept,
  When all things did appear
So perfectly harmonious,
  So bright and calm and clear.

V.

Then he spoke in woeful accents,
  As did such grief behoove,
Waving his lovely tentacles
  From softly silvered groove—
"I am the saddest thing alive
  Because I have to *move!*"

VI.

"To move!" said I; "to grow, you mean—
  The lot of living things!

But you grow in a pearly shell
  While others grow in wings,
In legs, fins, tails, beaks, horns, and scales,
  Proboscises, and stings!"

VII.

"No, no!" he cried, "it isn't *that*
  Which makes my grief and gloom,
In spite of summer sea and sky
  And irridescent bloom—
But when I grow I have to *move*,
  And build another room!

VIII.

"My little rooms! my little rooms!
  Each dear deserted shell!
So sweetly smooth, so softly bright,
  And fitting me so well!
I sob and grieve for each I leave
  But still I grow and swell!

IX.

I never can revisit them!
  Each step has made a wall!
I never can grow backward,
  And be young again and small!
I have to rise—to grow—to move!
  And I don't like it all!"

X.

I rose and wandered on a space,
  With thoughts too deep to tell;
And still, through all my pride of race,
  Above the billowy swell,
I heard the chambered nautilus
  A-weeping in his shell!

THE PIOUS PAWN

"I want to be good! I know that I should!"
  The little white pawn aspired;
"I try my best to outdo the rest
  In conduct to be desired.
I stand quite straight, I patiently wait,
  I keep to my own little square,
And I try to submit, when I'm taken from it,
  In hopes of a Heaven most fair."

The behavior you boast is that of a post!
  You may shine in your permanent groove,
But virtue, in chess, you will have to confess,
  Involves some discretion to move!
Your hopes may come true of that heaven in view,
  And again they may not—it's a guess!
But to be good, my dear, for anything here
  You have to know how to play chess!

THE DAILY SQUID

The Squid he has no implements
  To fight or run or think;
He has no fins, no wings, no feet,
  To swim, fly, run, or sink;
When he's attacked he can but hide
  In self-emitted ink.

SOME NORDICS

Swollen with pride of race they stand,
Exulting in their little land,
  The little tribe from whence they came;
Hoping to dominate the earth
With one high power, one highest worth,
  The Nordic name.

93

Only by what a race achieves,
By the world-useful works it leaves,
    Can any human stock lay claim
In the long list of those who give
The lasting gains by which we live
        To well-won fame.

And these? One branch of that great race
Winning indelible disgrace,
    The whole world's blame;
Showing for all historic time
In folly, cruelty and crime.
        Their Nordic shame.

TREE & SUN

The Tree said to the Sun
"Only and Perfect One!
Master of heat and light
Before whom the day is bright—
After whom follows the night;
In whose warmth we bloom and grow
And the sap streams richly flow;
Whose rays draw up the rain
To pour upon earth again;—
Rain, the delight of our leaves;—
O Sun! my strong heart grieves
That I may not better express
Our exquisite thankfulness—
Nor find fit voice to raise
In gratitude and praise—
That my soul no way can see
Rightly to worship Thee!"

Answered The Sun to the Tree—
"What is such praise to me?
Can you imagine The Sun
Caring that any one
Of the myriad plants of earth
Should appreciate his worth?
The joy of the glowing Sun

Is to feel that his work is done
That work in the life you know
Is to make things Grow! . . . .

Grow! If you wish to praise!
Let golden harvests blaze,
Let roses blossom as now,
The red fruit weigh on the bough
While green leaves bathe in the light
And the trees build height on height.

I am to be worshipped So—
Be what you are—And Grow!

WHY NATURE LAUGHS

In a very lonely forest,
　　Beside a lonely sea,
　I found an ancient woman once,
　　Beneath an ancient tree.

She was laughing there more wildly
　　Than I had ever dreamed.
At first she only sat and shook,
　　And then she rolled and screamed.

So I naturally accosted her,
　　And asked if I might share
The source of inward merriment
　　Which kept her screaming there.

She straightened up and looked at me
　　A moment—hardly more—
I seemed to make the lady laugh
　　Worse than she did before.

But finally, with gasps for breath,
　　And lips that twitched and curled,
Said she, "I'm Grandma Nature,
　　And I'm laughing at the World!"

95

"The world!" said I. "The world"
  said she,
  "Especially *your* half—
I used to rage and grieve for it,
  But now I only laugh.

I used to suffer fearfully
  To see your needless pain,
To see you mortify the flesh
  Because you had a brain.

To see you stultify the brain
  Because you had a soul,
To see you try to save a part
  By injuring the whole.

You stunt the brain with foolishness,
  You stunt the soul with lies,
You stunt the body with disease,
  And then you seek the skies.

You're sickly when you might be well,
  Fools when you might be wise,
And wicked when you might be good,
  Yet you expect the skies.

You hedge yourselves with needless walls,
  You bind with needless chains,
You drive away your natural joys,
  And court unnatural pains.

Why do I laugh?"—she shook again—
  "Oh dear! Oh dear! Oh dear!
Because your hell is such a farce,
  Your heaven is so near."

TWIGS

'Tis an amusing sight to see
The topmost twigs on a growing tree

96

Look down with freshly-worded scorn
On the boughs by which they are up-borne.
Below, beneath contempt, is sunk
The twigless mid-Victorian trunk;
While as for roots—how should they know
There must be roots for them to grow.

"We Twigs are Youth! Are Life!" they say,
"We are the World! We are Today!
This talk of boughs and trunk bark rough—
And tribal myth of roots—old stuff!"

The tree minds not the little dears;
It has had twigs in previous years.

THE FRONT WAVE

The little front wave ran up on the sand
   And frothed there, highly elated;
"I am the Tide!" cried the little front wave,
   "The waves before me are dated!"

QUEER PEOPLE

The people people work with best
   Are often very queer
The people people own by birth
   Quite shock your first idea;
The people people choose for friends
   Your common sense appall,
But the people people marry
   Are the queerest folks of all.

THE EARTH, THE WORLD, AND I

Child, said The Earth to me,
What can you do?

Why do you try?
Can you not see
That all you are and can ever be
Is the product of Heredity?—
Merely the outcome sure and true
Of other lives gone by?
Because your ancestors were such—
Back to primeval slime—
Therefore you ail and sin so much,
Therefore 'tis waste of time
For you to try to steer your course
Free of this cumulative force
Beast, plant, and rock your story runs
Back to the powers that swing the suns.
And can you disobey the laws
That move you from the primal cause?
Peace fretful child! be still!
And do my will!

Said I to The Earth—Dear Dirt—
Your remarks do not hurt,
Being peacefully perfectly true—
But the fact of my coming from you
Does not alter another, my dear—
This fact,—I am here
Evolution's long effort To Be—
Has resulted in me
And I hark with respect to your tones
As I would to my bones,
Should their feelings new utterance give—
Should they say "we allow you to live!"
Heredity? Yes, I admit
All you're claiming for it.
The "first cause" is still running your ranch,
But I'm a collateral branch!
In which the same power is set free
To be handled by me
You don't see it? No matter old friend
It's all one in the end.

Child, said The World to me,
What can you do?
Why do you try?

Can you not see
That all the effort you have spent
Is the product of Environment?—
That your surroundings govern you,
And circumstances nigh?
Because you're born in such an age,
Because you're taught from such a page,
Because your friends are so and so,
Therefore you act and feel and know
Just as you do. In vain you've tried
To throw this influence aside.
Fruit of your century and race,
Your family and dwelling place,
Your education work & friends—
You have no individual ends!
Peace fretful child! Be Still!
And do my will!

Said I to the World—I can take
No offense at the statements you make,
They are truthful as far as they go—
But there's much you don't know.
Your power you correctly define—
But you fail to see mine.
You make me, in part, it is true—
But my friend—who made you?
The environment strong on our race
Is not climate or place.
So much as each new demonstration
Of our social relation
Our strongest impressions we take
From conditions we make—
And when we don't like the effect,
We can change—can select,
Can unmake and remake and choose
The conditions we use!
Just think what the product will be
When I make you make me!

OUR WORLD

Is it so hard, for us, whose minds have grown,
From tribal limits, petty cousinship,

Out to a million counted nation's soul;
From pasture ranges, or a city wall,
To continental rule and ownership
To intercontinental talk and trade,
To travel and exchange from sea to sea;—
Is it so much, to ask mankind today
To spread a trifle wider, to enlarge
One further step, and see our trodden world,
Our well-known freely travelled modern world,
As One—as long each nation stood as one?

This is Our World, as little islands are;
Just a round place of land and water wide
For us to live on—where we have to live.
This is Mankind, Humanity, our Race,
And there is not more difference between
The highest haughtiest white man and the black,—
The lowest wildest savage in the wood,—
Than, in one nation, we may plainly see
Between wise courteous educated men
And their own savages in city slums.
No savage so degraded, so diseased,
So hopeless in accumulated shame,
As the ancestral paupers we have made,
With long black pedigrees of social crime.

If we can feel one nation, rich and poor,
Pious and vicious, ignorant and wise;
With high self-sacrifice of noblest life,
Long social service, fullest duty done,
By some; and also, piece and part of us,
Our criminal diseased degenerate ones;
Our feebleminded, idiot, insane,
Our weak poor half-developed backward class;
If all this makes a nation, and we stand
To guard and honor it, defend its rights,
Know it and love it as a living thing,—
Our Country! To serve which a man should live;
Our Country! To save which a man should die;—
If the plain ordinary common mind
Can hold a thought like this and live by it.
What hinders us from seeing this, Our World?

Our races are no wider set apart
By difference in stage of social growth
Than child from man, and as we love the child,
Feed it and teach it, wait for it to grow,
So should grown races help the little ones
By transcendent aid of social power;
Assisted evolution, that which lifts
A people over centuries of change,
Giving to all, in rapid smooth advance,
The benefits attained by one alone.

Some nations are superior? Agreed.
So are some persons to the rest of us.
No nation has appeared where all the folk
Stand flat and even as a level beach,
Identical as grain on grain on sand.
But in our nations we can clearly see
That statesmanship and learning, power and skill,
Appear and grow in service to the rest,
And only so. Superiority
Means but the Great Man's Burden, the high law
Of duty to the less—*noblesse oblige.*

Our world, with a new spirit, a new hope flag,
Flag of the white orb, belted with the red
Of our one blood, our human brotherhood,
Centered supreme in a blue field of stars;
Our world, Our Country, Our Humanity,
No one land over all, but all for one
And one for all, in widest comradeship;
This gives at last room for the human soul,
Room to fulfill ambition's highest hope,
Love's deepest service, wisdom's widest power;
Something to live for, fully satisfied,
And facing death with utter unconcern,
So that, in living, we have served Our World.

OUR WORLD
AN INTERNATIONAL HYMN

I.

Proud each nation's noble story,
  Home defended, warriors bold,

101

Prouder still their common glory
  When in peace our world we hold.
Sovereign states whose high devotion
  Long each country spent alone.
Joining over land and ocean
  For the world they make their own.

II.

World of peace, where wealth and beauty
  Safe at last may spread and grow,
Strong in justice, clear in duty,
  Wise in all the good we know.
Freedom for our lives unfolding,
  Honor for all service done,
Highest gain each land is holding,
  Ours, when all the world is one.

III.

Light at last on our confusion,
  Clear at last our human plan,
Bright and free from all illusion
  Shines the rising hope of man.
Crown of all the climbing ages,
  Goal of all the road we trod,
Grows on earth a social body
  Worthy of the soul of God.

THE FLAG OF PEACE

Men have long fought for their flying flags,
  They have died those flags to save;
Their long staves rest on the shattered breast,
  They are planted deep in the grave.
Now the world's new flag is streaming wide,
  Far flying wide and high,
It shall cover the earth from side to side
  As the rainbow rings the sky.

102

The flag of the day when men shall stand
    For service, not for fight;
When every race in every land,
    Shall join for the world's delight;
When all our flags shall blend in one,
    And all our wars shall cease,
'Neath the new flag! The true flag!
    The rainbow flag of peace.

On a field of white that bow above
    Shall arch the world across,
And all the colors that we love
    Glow there without a loss.
Orange and green in union new,
    Proud gold and violet fair,
With world-beloved red white and blue
    Shall shine together there.

Green for the earth that holds us one,
    All blue of sky and sea,
And the golden hue of that great sun
    In whose light our life must be.
Red for the blood of brotherhood,
    White for the soul's release,—
The new flag! The true flag!
    The rainbow flag of peace!

SONG FOR THE WORLD'S FLAG

As the green earth shines in the star-filled sky,
    Our white world shines on the blue;
Each free land with its star on high,
All held close by the crimson tie
    Of one blood, strong and true.

(Chorus)
Union! Union! States of all the World!
    Union widening fast!
One is the Power that made mankind,
One the human heart is! One the human mind!
    One is the World at last!

White blood of progress, blue blood of pride,
  Black blood of service and cheer,
Yellow, red, or brown man, white man beside,
Room for them all in the world so wide—
  Red blood of brotherhood here.

(Chorus)
Union! Union! States of all the World!
  Union widening fast!
One is the Power that made mankind,
One the human heart is! One the human mind!
  One is the world at last!

STATE SOVEREIGNTY

Said the solemn self-important Sovereign State
  To the Nation which enables it to live,
"We're supreme in our inborn superiority—
You are nothing but a delegate authority
  Which the states that met to make you deigned to give!"

(Now whatever such a theory may mean
It belongs to the original thirteen:
And not to one this nation, as a nation
Established in auriferous temptation.)

Said the haughty self-assertive Sovereign State,
  "We shall govern here exactly as we please;
If we dislike a certain nationality
We repudiate your treaty-made equality,
  And discriminate against them at our ease."

(Now whatever California may do
To the Chinaman, the Dago and the Jew,
She's facing here a different condition—
Japan is quite another proposition!)

THE KINGDOM

"Where is Heaven?" asked the Person.
I want Heaven—to enjoy it;

I want Heaven, recompensing
For the evils I have suffered—
All the terrible injustice,
All the foolish waste and hunger—
Where is Heaven? Can I get there?"

Then the Priest expounded Heaven:
"Heaven is a place for dead men;
After you are dead you'll find it,
If"—and here the Priest was earnest—
"*If* you do the things I tell you—
Do exactly what is ordered!
It will cost you quite a little—
You must pay a price for Heaven—
You must pay before you enter."

Am I sure of what I'm getting?"
Asked the mean, suspicious Person.
"What you urge is disagreeable;
What you ask is quite expensive;
Am I sure of getting Heaven?"

Then the Priest prepared a potion,
Made of Concentrated Ages,
Made of Many Mingled Feelings—
Highest Hope and Deepest Terror—

Mixed our best and worst together,
Reverence and Love and Service,
Coward Fear and rank Self-Interest—
Gave him this when he was little,

Pumped it in before the Person
Could examine his prescription.
So the Person, thus instructed,
Now believed the things he told him;
Paid the price as he was able,
Died—the Priest said, went to Heaven—
None came back to contradict him!

* * *

"We want Heaven," said the People;
"We believe in God and Heaven;

105

Where God is, there must be Heaven;
God is Here—and this is Heaven."

Then they saw the earth was lovely;
Life was sweet, and love eternal;
Then they learned the joy of living,
Caught a glimpse of what Life might be,
What it could be—should be—would be—
When the People chose to have it!

Then they bought no further tickets
Of the sidewalk speculators;
They no longer gave their children
The "spring medicine" of Grandma.
They said, "We will take no chances
Of what happens after dying;

We perceive that Human Beings,
Wise, and sweet, and brave, and tender,
Strong, and beautiful, and noble,
Living peaceably together,
In a universal garden
With the Sciences for Soldiers,

With the Allied Arts for Angels
With the Crafts and Trades for Servants,
With all Nature for the Teacher,
And all People for the Students,
Make a very pleasant Heaven.
We can see and understand it,
We believe we'd really like some,
Now we'll set to work and make it!"

So they set to work together,
In the Faith that rests on Knowledge,
In the Hope that's born of Wisdom,
In the Love that grows with Practise—
And proceeded to make Heaven.

And God smiled. He had been tired
Of the everlasting dead men,
Of the hungry, grasping, dead men;

He had always wanted live ones—
Wanted them to build the Kingdom!

THIS LOVELY EARTH

When you are young and all the world is new,
When you are old and it is home to you,
And all through life, in pleasure, hope and pain,
Laughing in sunlight, resting under rain,
Taking all weathers at their welcome worth,
To love and love and love this lovely earth!

HAPPINESS

That which mankind from birth forever seeks,
    All men, all women, in the dark or light,
This common voice must be where Nature speaks,
    This common need is surely proven right.

Deep in the human heart lies one demand,
    One simple natural longing all confess,
We ask of life, of love, of God's high hand,
    This one thing only—perfect happiness!

THERE ARE THOSE WHO CAN SEE

There are those who can see what has happened before
    If it came at a pace that was slow,
They know it the best and believe it the more
    If it happened long ages ago.

There are those who can see things that happen today,
    If they shine like a Kohinoor gem,
If they fall upon all in a violent way,
    And especially, fall upon them.

But those who can see through the future ahead,
  See great truths over things that are small,
See the ages unborn, not the days that are dead,
  These are they who give help to us all.

BEGIN NOW

O, never mind what the world has done
    Before,
As a matter of fact, we've just begun—
    No more!
The glory of life is ours to take;
The world we want is for us to make;
The loveliest faith of all the lands
    Is true,
And the building of heaven is in our hands
    To do!

THANKFULNESS

Not one sorrow or distress
Lets us off from thankfulness—
Not one sorrow—no, not twenty!
There is joy abroad in plenty!

Not one hidden shame or sin
Ought to keep our gladness in—
Never mind what has been done—
There is time for every one!

If your life was long and black
And death gains upon your track—
Grieve not so, for after all
That whole wrongness was but small!

In the all embracing right
It will be forgotten quite;
In God's goodness swallowed free
Like an inkspot in the sea!

A Chant Royal

I.

Waken, O Women, to the trumpet sound
   Greeting our day of long sought liberty;
Gone are the ages that have held us bound
   Beneath a master, now we stand as he,
Free for world-service unto all mankind,
Free of the dragging chains that used to bind,
   The sordid labor, the unnoticed woe,
   The helpless shame, the unresisted blow,
Submission to our owner's least command—
   No longer pets or slaves are we, for lo!
Women are free at last in all the land.

II.

Long was the stony road our feet have found
   From that darl past to the new world we see,
Each step with heavy hindrance hemmed around,
   Each door to freedom closed with bolt and key
Our feet with old tradition all entwined,
Untrained, uneducated, uncombined,
   We had to fight old faiths of long ago,
   And in our households find our dearest foe,
Against the world's whole weight we had to stand
   Till came the day it could no more say no—
Women are free at last in all the land.

III.

Around us prejudice, emotion-drowned,
   Rose like a flood and would not let us free;
Women themselves, soft-bred and silken gowned,
   Historic shame have won by their mad plea
To keep their own subjection; with them lined
All evil forces of the world we find;
   No crime so brazen and no vice so low
   But fought us, with inertia blind and slow,
And ignorance beneath its darkling brand
   With these we strove and still must strive, although
Women are free at last in all the land.

109

IV.

The serving squaw, the peasant, toil-embrowned
   The household drudge, no honor and no fee—
For these we now see women world renowned,
   In art and science, work of all degree.
She whom world progress had left far behind
Now has the secret of full life divined,
   Her largest service gladly to bestow;
   Great is the gain since ages far below,
In honored labor, both of head and hand
   Now may her power and genius clearly show
Women are free at last in all the land.

V.

Long years of effort to her praise rebound
   To such high courage all may bend the knee,
Beside her brother, with full freedom crowned,
   Mother and wife and citizen is she,
Queen of her soul and body, heart and mind,
Strong for the noble service God designed,
   See now the marching millions, row by row,
   With steady eyes and faces all aglow,
They come! they come! a glad triumphant band.—
   Roses and laurels in their pathway strew—
Women are free at last in all the land!

ENVOI.

Sisters! we now must change the world we know
To one great garden where the child may grow.
   New freedom means new duty broad and grand.
To make a better world and hold it so
   Women are free at last in all the land.

HAPPY DAY

We want to vote for a bright tomorrow,
Dawn of hope and end of sorrow!

Happy day! Happy day! Happy day! For the world!
Vote for the men who will do their duty,
Country's good and city's beauty!
    Happy day! Happy day! Happy day! For the world!

           Chorus:
See us coming all together! Hoo-ray! Hoo-ray!
And hand in hand we'll take our stand
      To win the vote for women!
        Today! Today!
      To win the vote for women!
        Today! Today!
      To win the vote for women!

We want to vote as wives and mothers!
With our husbands, fathers, brothers!
    Happy day! Happy day! Happy day! For the world!

To save the home and the children in it!
Work to do, so now begin it!
    Happy day! Happy day! Happy day! For the world!

We are not fools and we are not crazy;
We're not bad, corrupt, nor lazy:
    Happy day! Happy day! Happy day! For the world!

We'll use our power when the power is given;
Make this world more fit to live in!
    Happy day! Happy day! Happy day! For the world!

In Honor, Truth and Right our trust is;
Give us Freedom! Give us Justice!
    Happy day! Happy day! Happy day! For the world!

The People's Voice is Freedom's axis!
All should vote who pay their taxes!
    Happy day! Happy day! Happy day! For the world!

NOBLESSE OBLIGE

I.

I was well born . . . .
A wise, free maiden grew to womanhood,

111

Guiding and training her young life for me;
With splendid body, vigorous and strong;
A heart well used; a brain of fluent power.
She gloried in the crown of motherhood;
And chose a father fit to share her reign;
And the two, reverent, passionate, devout,
Gave me my entailed heritage full store,
The better for their loyal stewardship.

II.

I was well trained.
My schooling opened with my baby eyes,
Was breathed with my first breathing. Purest air,
All sunlight and sweet winds and waves were mine.
Life came to me translated to the tongue
That I could understand and profit by.
I drank in wisdom with unconscious sense;
Long centuries of labor, glorified
Into profound simplicity by art,
Grew mine in brief, bright hours of playtime there.
They taught me—all who ever lived before—
Taught me free use of body, use of brain,
And sent me forth a full developed man,
With easy mastery of his powers.

III.

And I am rich.
I revel in immeasurable wealth;
Sitting, aweary of one day's delight
And picturing my endless treasures;
Those I have counted—those I draw from now—
And those beyond exhaustion still to come:
Running my fingers through the heaps of gems
And tossing them, for gifts, till hands are tired.
So rich, so rich beyond all fear or doubt
That no desire for my own private need
Can ever enter my untroubled mind.
I am secure as rolls the easy sun,
And there remains but this: To Act! To Do!

IV.

Shall I not work?
I, who am wholly free and have no care;

112

I, with such press of power at my command;
I, who stand here in front of human life
And feel the push of all the heaving past
Straining against my hand!
Immortal life,
Eternal, indestructible, the same
In flower, and beast, and savage, now in me
Urges and urges to expression new.
Work? Shall I take from those blind laboring years
Their painful fruit and not contribute now
My share of gifts so easy to our time?
Shall I receive so much, support the weight
Of age-long obligation, and not turn
In sheerest pride, and strive to set my mark
A little past the record made before?
Shall it be said, "He took, from all the world,
Of its accumulated countless wealth,
As much as he could hold, and never gave!
Spiritless Beggar! Pauper! Parasite!"

Life is not long enough to let me work
As I desire. But all the years will hold
Shall I pour forth. Perhaps it may be mine
To do some deed was never done before
And ease my obligation to the world!

WHERE WOMEN MEET

Where women meet!—The village well
Was once their place; the convent cell
   For centuries asleep and slow,
   Gave all the grouping they could know
Or market-place, to buy and sell.

Now year by year their numbers swell
In crowded halls, 'neath chairman's bell;
   To aid the weak, to lift the low,
   To urge the right—these efforts show
    Where women meet.

New light, our shadows to dispel—
New power beyond all parallel

From motherhood combined shall flow
Helping our stumbling race to grow,—
And a clean happy world will tell
Where women meet.

To the Indifferent Woman

You who are happy in a thousand homes,
Or overworked therein, to a dumb peace;
Whose souls are wholly centered in the life
Of that small group you personally love;
Who told you that you need not know or care
About the sin and sorrow of the world?

Do you believe the sorrow of the world
Does not concern you in your little homes?—
That you are licensed to avoid the care
And toil for human progress, human peace,
And the enlargement of our power of love
Until it covers every field of life?

The one first duty of all human life
Is to promote the progress of the world
In righteousness, in wisdom, truth and love;
And you ignore it, hidden in your homes,
Content to keep them in uncertain peace,
Content to leave all else without your care.

Yet you are mothers! and a mother's care
Is the first step toward friendly human life,
Life where all nations in untroubled peace
Unite to raise the standard of the world
And make the happiness we seek in homes
Spread everywhere in strong and fruitful love.

You are content to keep that mighty love
In its first steps forever; the crude care
Of animals for mate and young and homes,
Instead of pouring it abroad in life,
Its mighty current feeding all the world
Till every human child can grow in peace.

You cannot keep your small domestic peace
Your little pool of undeveloped love,
While the neglected, starved, unmothered world
Struggles and fights for lack of mother's care,
And its tempestuous, bitter, broken life
Beats in upon you in your selfish homes.

We all may have our homes in joy and peace
When woman's life, in its rich power of love
Is joined with man's to care for all the world.

ONE GIRL OF MANY

1.

One girl of many. Hungry from her birth
Half-fed. Half-clothed. Untaught of woman's worth.
In joyless girlhood working for her bread.
At each small sorrow wishing she were dead,
Yet gay at little pleasures. Sunlight seems
Most bright & warm where it most seldom gleams.

2.

One girl of many. Tawdry dress and old;
And not enough beneath to bar the cold.
The little that she had misspent because
She had no knowledge of our nature's laws.
Thinking in ignorance that it was best
To wear a stylish look, and—bear the rest.

3.

One girl of many. With a human heart.
A woman's too; with nerves that feel the smart
Of each new pain as keenly as your own.
The old ones, through long use, have softer grown.
And yet in spite of use she holds the thought
Of might-be joys more than, perhaps, she ought.

4.

One girl of many. But the fault is here;
Though she to all the others was so near;
One difference there was, which made a change.
No wrong thing, surely. Consequence most strange!
Alike in birth. Alike in life's rough way.
She, through no evil, was more fair than they.

5.

So came the offer, "Leave this story cold
Where you may drudge and starve till you are old.
Come! I will give you rest. And food. And fire.
And fair apparel to your heart's desire;
Shelter. Protection. Kindness. Peace & Love.
Has your life anything you hold above?"

6.

And she had *not*. In all her daily sight
There shone no vestige of the color *White*.
She had seen nothing in her narrow life
To make her venerate the title "Wife."
She knew no *reason* why the thing was wrong;
And instinct grows debased in ages long.

7.

All things that she had ever yet desired
All dreams that her starved girlhood's heart had fired
All that life held of yet unknown delight
Shone, to her ignorance, in colors bright.
Shone near at hand and sure. If she had *known!*
But she was ignorant. She was alone.

8.

And so she—sinned. I think we call it sin.
And found that every step she took therein
Made sinning easier and conscience weak.
And there was never one who cared to speak

A word to guide and warn her. If there were
I fear such help were thrown away on her.

9.

Only one girl of many. Of the street.
In lowest depths. The story grows unmeet
For wellbred ears. Sorrow and sin and shame
Over and over till the blackened name
Sank out of sight without a hand to save.
Sin, shame, and sorrow. Sickness, & the grave.

10.

Only one girl of many. Tis a need
Of man's existence to repeat the deed.
Social necessity. Men cannot live
Without what these disgraceful creatures give.
Black shame. Dishonor. Misery & Sin.
And men find needed health & life therein.

THE DEPARTING HOUSEMAID

The housewife is held to her labors
    By three great powers—
Love, that poureth like water
    Through hours and hours.

Duty, high as the heavens,
    Deep as the sea—
These, and the great compeller,
    Necessity.

Duty holds her to housework,
    Sin to be free;
These are the bonds of the housewife—
    They bind not me!

The man is spurred to his labors
    Of plow or sword,

117

By two of the great incentives—
    Pride and Reward.

He in his work finds glory,
    Height after height;
He in his work finds riches,
    Gain and delight.

Triumph of world-wide conquest—
    Profit in fee;
These spur man to his labors—
    They spur not me!

I am the lowest of labor,
    Ignorant, strong.
They on my ignorance reckoned,
    Held me thus long.

Lately I grow to discover
    Life's broader way:
Nothing to hold me or spur me—
    Why should I stay?

THE PAST PARENT & THE COMING CHILD

Turn now and look your parent in the face—
That face long misled with reverence compelled
Let us revere the truth and not a veil—
Off with it! Let the present lift its head
And see and know and judge the dwindling Past.
The garments of tradition hide the shape—
Which we were taught to honor as sublime—
Glory and strength of hallowed Golden Age—
Mythical Heroes merging into gods—
But keen eyed science with is newfound light
Pierces the myths and shows us—O forlorn!—
The low browed savage—and the chinless ape
Smaller than we—and weaker—and less wise—
Slow growing through a thousand senseless sins—
Forced on, reluctant, up historic stairs,
Resisting, holding back, delaying Time.

118

Holding Us back! Trying from age to age
To keep us still delinquent as itself!
To keep the Present subject to the Past!
O blessed light of truth that sets us free—
Free of those chains that drag along the years.
Let us forgive—forget and turn our face
For good and all ahead! And what awaits—
What looms so large—what grows, so fast, ahead—
O love and Pride! The Future's splendid child!

BODY OF MINE

Body of mine! That once was fair—
   Soft, smooth, and fair—
Glad was my soul in its garment fine,
Glad of the crown of shining hair.
   Color of roses, eyes of the sea—
   Glad and proud was my soul of thee,
      Body of mine!

Body of mine! That once was young,
   Slim, swift, and young.
Glad was my heart with youth's rich wine,
Spring in the footstep—song on the tongue,
   Joylight and lovelight shining on me—
   Glad and gay was my heart in thee,
      Body of mine!

Body of mine that now grows old—
   Thin, dry, and old—
Flowers may wither and pets may pine,
Fire of passion grow palely cold—
   But the living world is the frame of me—
   Heart and soul are not found in thee—
      Body of mine!

The world, the sky, and the work of our hands,
   Wonderful work of our hands!
Clothe my soul in a form divine
Young forever to all demands
   Ageless and deathless and boundless and free

Glory and joy do I find in thee,
Body of mine!

MATRIATISM

Small is the thought of "Fatherland,"
With all its pride and worth;
With all its history of death;
Of fire and sword and wasted breath—
By the great new thought which quickeneth—
The thought of "Mother Earth."
Man fights for wealth and rule and pride,
For the "name" that is his alone;
Comes woman, wakening to her power,
Comes woman, opening the hour
That sees life as one growing flower,
All children as her own.

Fathers have fought for their Fatherland
With slaughter and death and dearth,
But mothers, in service and love's increase,
Will labor together for our release,
From a war-stained past to a world at peace,
Our fair, sweet Mother Earth.

FULL MOTHERHOOD

There are children many—this child is mine;
    Shall I love them all or only one?
What motherhood is the world's design?

Born of a known and honored line,
    Blossom of love, an only son—
There are children many, this child is mine;

But what of the others who starve and pine,
    Where no wise mother tasks are done?
What motherhood is the world's design?

Unless my baby is fair and fine
   The game is lost and the race not run;
There are children many, this child is mine.

Unless we love both mine and thine,
   Heaven on earth can come for none—
What motherhood is the world's design?

We must care for all with a love divine;
   Only so may the game be won;
There are children many—this child is mine—
   Full motherhood is the world's design.

To Mothers

In the name of your ages to anguish!
In the name of the curse and the stain!
By the strength of your sorrow I call you
By the power of your pain!

We are mothers. Through us in our bondage,
Through us with a brand in the face,
Be we fettered with gold or with iron,
Through us comes the race.

With the weight of all sin on our shoulders,
Midst the serpents of shame ever curled,
We have sat, unresisting, defenseless,—
Making the men of the world!

We were ignorant long, and our children
Were besotted and brutish and blind,
King-driven, priest-ridden,—who are they
Our children—mankind.

We were kept for our beauty, our softness,
Our sex,—what reward do ye find?
We transmit, must transmit, being mothers,
What we are to mankind!

As the mother so follow the children!
No nation, wise, noble and brave,
Ever sprang,—though the father had freedom,—
From the mother,—a slave.

Look now at the world as ye find it!
Blench not! Truth is kinder than lies!
Look now at the world—see it suffer!
Listen now to its cries!

See the people who suffer, all people!
All humanity wasting its powers!
In a hand to hand struggle—death dealing—
All children of ours!

The blind millionaire—the blind harlot—
The blind preacher leading the blind—
Only think of the pain, how it hurts them!
Our little blind babies—mankind!

Shall we bear it? We mothers who love them.
Can we bear it? We mothers who feel
Every pang of our babes and forgive them
Every sin when they kneel?

Little stumbling world! You have fallen!
You are crying in darkness and fear!
Wait, darling, your mother is coming!
Hush, darling, your mother is here!

We are here like an army with banners
The great flag of our freedom unfurled!
With us rests the fate of the nations,
For we make the world!

Dare ye sleep while your children are calling?
Dare ye wait while they clamor unfed?
Dare ye pray in the proud pillared churches
While they suffer for bread?

If the farmer hath sinned he shall answer,
If he check thee laugh back at his powers!

Shall a mother be kept from her children?
These people are ours!

They are ours! He is ours, for we made him!
In our arms he has nestled and smiled!
Shall we, the world-mothers, be hindered
By the freaks of a child?

Rise now in the power of The Woman!
Rise now in the power of our need!
The world cries in hunger and darkness!
We shall light! We shall feed!

In the name of our ages of anguish!
In the name of the curse and the slain!
By the strength of our sorrow we conquer!
In the power of our pain!

DARK AGES

I lived, and bore.
And, though I died,
So that I lived to bear—
My daughter lived and bore.

THE SOURCE

Behind us lies a long forgetfulness—
    Past upon past deep buried in the brain;
No memories penetrate those ages old,
Lift the uncounted curtains, fold on fold,
    And let us see our earliest days again.

Could they—what wonder, interest, delight,
    Clouded with shame for those dark, stumbling years,
In tracing up that long unbroken line,
That slow development of life divine,
    From beast to man—the triumph and the tears!

123

Yet always one unfailing source of power—
    However low we go or high we come,
However crude or cruel, weak or blind,
    Through every change, in every age, we find
      The Mother and the Baby and the Home.

I AM HUMAN

I was deprived in childhood—robbed of my birthright fair!
I have never had what belonged to me, and they stole from my scanty
    share.
I have suffered—oh, how I have suffered!
    Outrage and loss and pain!
Are the Heavens deaf? Is God a lie, that such black wrongs remain?
What matter! ah, what matter! what shall it count to me?
These things that "I" have suffered—what is that I to "We"?
We—We who are Human—life that is old as Time—
Life of the blended nations; life that is now sublime!
Life that has buried billions and poured forth billions more—
Life that has suffered for ages, and rejoices as never before!
Life that carries its evils, disease and sorrow and sin.
By the power of eternal progress—the progress we all are in;
That bears with its weak and little, its errors of church and state,
By the strength and truth and virtue of its all uncounted great!
Human! am I not Human! Is not the world's life mine?
Shall the fate of a single creature disturb that calm divine?

The little "I" that suffered was but a part of me—
A fraction slight as a wavelet light on a world-encircling sea.
I may sorrow for it, as for others; there is pain man should not bear,
But the joy and the power of Human Life makes that an easy care.
We may mend it and remove it—we may make all men glad,
So soon as we turn our common power to help the separate sad,
When we lift our soul from the microscope of personal concern
And let the light of Human Love have room to shine and burn.

I have rejoiced through the ages. Since life was made. I live,
In the wealth of power and the peace of power and the joy that power
    can give.
I have climbed the way of the ages in the steps that must be trod;
And I stand of the very threshold of a world that knows its God.

Hark! was some one crying? Does some one yet complain?
We cannot go on to our splendid day while any in want remain.
Hush! It is easy to aid you; the power and the instant will.
Wisdom and limitless love are mine; bring me your cup to fill!
Come! To riches and beauty, and freedom that none can bar—
Were you myself a thousand times—see what you really are!

Good Will

As the strong sweet light of the morning,
As the strong sweet air of the sea,
As the strong sweet music of the wind among the leaves
Comes the voice of our good will to a weary world that grieves,
Crying "Be glad! Be free!"

Waste no sorrow on the days that lie behind you,
Waste no fear upon the days that rise before,
Waste no time in fierce complaining that the world is thus and so,
The world is ours my brothers, and we make it as we go.
Make it more and more.

Truth is shining in our souls like the morning,
Power is swelling within us like the sea,
Love is rising like a mighty wind that sweeps disease away
Love that shall be in the future, love that is, that is today,
Brothers! Be glad! Be free!

The Coming Day

As the strong, sweet light of the morning,
    As the strong, sweet air of the sea,
As the strong, sweet music of the air among the leaves,
    Comes the voice of our goodwill to a weary world that grieves,
        Crying, Be glad! Be free!

Youth is shining within us like the morning,
    Power is rising within us like the sea,
Love is coming like the mighty wind that sweeps disease away—

Love that shall be in the future—love that is, that is to-day,
  Brothers! Be glad! Be free!

FROM TWO ALBUMS

1.

Be strong! Be brave! Be absolutely true!
  As you would wish your wife, be pure!
  Deserve your own best honor, and be sure
That all whom you love best will honor you!

2.

So fair the page, so beautiful the lilies
  We dread to see black ink such whiteness strewing:
And yet, though pure the soul, though good the will is,
  There is no life for us except in doing!

THIS IS THE YEAR

Forget all the Buried and welcome the Born!
  These that are coming are Real!
Plough for the Beautiful Dream of the Corn—
  Build the Ideal!

Changeless the Past, but the Future is ours—
  Open for us to endow;
Fruit of our purposes, proof of our powers—
  Work for it Now!

All we desire is for us to create—
  Here in our hands, here!
This is the Hour that is Never Too Late!
  This is The Year!

THOUGHTS AND FACTS

Once we thought the world was flat,
   What of that?
It was just as globose then,
Under unbelieving men,
As our later folk have found it,
By success in running round it.
   What we think may guide our acts,
   But it does not alter facts.

We thought women made and meant
   For man's content;
Rib-made secondary things,
Not the stuff for priests and kings.
Greatly we admired the plan
Of "God's last best gift to man."
Now we're learning, somewhat late,
Female life to antedate
   These old-world man-made chimeras,
   By some geologic eras.

Long the life stream held its own,
   Hers alone.
That first form, through ages dim,
Slowly has developed him.
Late he came, with little stir,
As God's last best gift to her.
   What he thinks may guide his acts,
   But it does not alter facts.

THE HUMAN LAW

We watch the solemn courses of the stars,
And feel the swell of reverence and praise,
Even though some may fall: . . .

      We watch the birds,
The small birds, finding each her food and mate;
Nest-building, happy, busy, free from care,
Even though some may starve: . . .

127

We see in these
The smooth fulfillment of their nature's law;
They are content and calm and good to see,
Because of this fulfillment; they are true.
And we? Have we no law? May we not show
That power in peace, that happiness in work,
That rich contentment in our share of life,—
Even though some may fail? . . .
What is our law?

Truth: To be true: To hold oneself in line
With the uplifting forces of the world,
That lift us as they lifted continents;
Truth to one's work.

Courage: The courage that can stand alone
Against the doubt and hate of millions here,
Against the million millions of the past,
Against one's own distrust.
Courage that stands.

Love: To wish well to all the human race;
To will toward happiness for every one.
To feel, to guard, to give—
Love actual.

Work: Not pay-earning, but the outflow wide
Of one's best powers in special services,
Those subtle services that build the world,
Each for the others, organized and strong.
This is the Human Law. So we should live,
Each honestly fulfilling one's own task,
In love and courage; seeing in that work
The smooth fulfillment of our nature's law,
Even though some may fail. . . .

THE PURPOSE

Serene she sat, full grown in human power,
Established in the service of the world,
Full-hearted, rich, strong with the age's life,

Wise with the womanhood of centuries,
With broad still brows and deep eyes lit beneath
With fire of inextinguishable love,
In beauty which the study of a life
Would fail to measure—beauty as of hills
Or the heart-stilling wonder of the sea.

Then came her lovers, awed and passionate,
With naught to offer she had not as much
Save only—manhood. Lovers made by God
To offer to her final power of choice
Their natural tribute of diverging gifts,
The man's inherent variance of growth,
That she, by choosing, build a better race.
Theirs the resistless longing to fulfill
Their nature's primal law at any cost,
The one great purpose of their parted life;
Love their first cause, love their determined end.

So she, from ardent, emulous appeal,
After the inner ruling of her heart
Chose him of all best mated to herself,
Best qualified to glorify The Child—
For this was she made woman—not for him.

THE PRIMAL POWER

Would ye plant the world with new-made men?
   A race new-born, a race unstained?
Clothed in flesh that hath no flaw,
One with nature, one with law,
   Strong-souled, clear-brained?

This may motherhood achieve,
   Full-grown mothers brave and free,
Splendid bodies trained and strong,
Hearts that ache for human wrong,
   Eyes that can see.

Learning new their primal power,
   A reign forgot, a crown disowned—

Rising from their prison blind,
Pets and servants of mankind—
    Re-born, re-throned.

Theirs the power beyond appeal
    To choose the good, reject the base;
So shall all degenerate blood
Die, forbidden fatherhood—
    So rise our race!

Two Prayers

Only for these I pray,
    Pray with assurance strong;
Light to discover the way,
    Power to follow it long.

Let me have Light to see,
    Light to be sure and know,
When the road is clear to me
    Willingly I go.

Let me have Power to do,
    Power of the brain and nerve,
Though the task is heavy and new
    Willingly I will serve.

My prayers are lesser than three,
    Nothing I pray but two;
Let me have light to see,
    Let me have Power to do.

Between Past & Future

In the path from the past to the future—
    in the years between age and youth—
I met three angels hand in hand
    (A flower-lit meadow—a sunkissed land)—

130

Love—Joy—Truth.

From my heart rise thanks to heaven—
　From my eyes the glad tears fall!
Love that changes from day to day—
Joy that ranges yet still doth stay—
　　Truth that is all in all.

Whatever Is

Whatever is we only know
As in our minds we find it so;
　　No staring fact is half so clear
　　As one dim, preconceived idea—
No matter how the fact may glow.

Vainly may Truth her trumpet blow
To stir our minds; like heavy dough
　　They stick to what they think—won't hear
　　Whatever is.

Our ancient myths in solid row
Stand up—we simply have to go
　　And choke each fiction old and dear
　　Before the modest facts appear;
Then we may grasp, reluctant, slow,
　　Whatever is.

Part Three
The Artist

WINGS

A sense of wings—
    Soft downy wings and fair—
Great wings that whistle as they sweep
Along the still gulfs—empty, deep—
    Of thin blue air.

    Doves' wings that follow,
      Doves' wings that fold,
    Doves' wings that flutter down
      To nestle in your hold.

    Doves' wings that settle,
      Doves' wings that rest,
    Doves' wings that brood so warm
      Above the little nest.

    Larks' wings that rise and rise,
    Climbing the rosy skies—
      Fold and drop down
      To birdlings brown.

Light wings of wood-birds, that once scarce believes
    Moved in the leaves.

    The quick, shy flight
    Of wings that flee in fright—
    A start as swift as light—
    Only the shaken air
    To tell that wings were there.

Broad wings that beat for many days
Above the land wastes and the water ways;
    Beating steadily on and on,
      Through dark and cold,
      Through storms untold,
Till the far sun and summer land is won.

And wings—
     Wings that unfold
With such wide sweep before your would-be hold—
Such glittering sweep of whiteness—sun on snow—
Such mighty plumes—strong-ribbed, strong-webbed—
     strong-knit to go
          From earth to heaven!
          Hear the air flow back
          In their wide track!
     Feel the sweet wind these wings displace
          Beat on your face!
See the great arc of light like rising rockets trail
          They leave in leaving—
          They avail—
          These wings—for flight!

WORSHIP

     How does it feel?—
     The drawing of the magnet on the steel?
     All else gives way;
     To rivets bold, no bars delay.
     Called in that overwhelming hour,
     From far and near they fly and cling.
     Allied, united, christening;
     And the great pulsing currents flow
     Through each small scattered scrap below.
     Scattered no more.
     One with that all compelling core;
     One absolute, one all alive with power.

     How does it feel?—
     The swift obedient utmost flight
     Of radiant sky-wide waves of light,
     Pancouriens of the central sun
     Crossing a million miles as one—
     Still going—going—
     Limitless joy that needs no knowing
     Each last least flickering ray
     One with the Heart of Day.

THE ARTIST

Here one of us is born, made as a lens,
Or else to lens-shape cruelly smooth-ground,
To gather light, the light that shines on all,
In concentrated flame it glows, pure fire,
With light a hundredfold, more light for all.

Come and receive, take with the eye or ear,
Take and be filled, illumined, overflowed;
Then go and shine again, your whole work lit,
Your whole heart warm and luminous and glad;
Go shine again—and spread the gladness wide;

Happy the lens! To gather skies of light
And focus it, making the splendor there!
Happy all we who are enriched therewith,
And redistribute ever, swift and far.

The artist is the intermediate lens
Of God, and so best gives Him to the world,
Intensified, interpreted, to us.

MY VIEW, 1881.

From my high window the outlooker sees
   The whole wide southern sky,
Fort Hill is in the distance smiling green,
With ordinary houses thick between,
   And scanty passers by.

Our street is flat, ungraded, little used,
   The sidewalks grown with grass,
And just across, a fenceless open lot,
Covered with ash-heaps, where the sun shines hot
   On bits of broken glass.

It's hard on Nature, blotting her fair face
   With such discourteous deeds,
But one short season gives her time enough

137

To softly cover up the outlines rough
　　With merciful thick weeds.

Then numerous most limited back-yards,
　　One thick with fruit trees, overgrown with vines,
But most of them are rather bare and small,
With board and picket fences, running all
　　In parallel straight lines.

Hardly a brilliant prospect you will think,
　　The common houses, scanty passers by,
Bare lot thick-strown with cinder-heaps and shards,
And small monotonous township of back-yards—
　　Stop—you forget the sky!

LITTLE LEAFY BROTHERS

Little leafy brothers! You can feel
Warmth o' the sun,
Cool sap streams run,
The slow soft nuzzling creep
Of roots sent deep,
And a close-anchored flowing
In winds smooth blowing.
And in the spring! The spring!
When the stars sing—
The world's love in you grows
Into the rose.

Little hairy brothers! You can feel
The kind sun too;
Winds play with you,
Water is live delight—
In your own swift flight
Of wings or leaping feet
Life rushes sweet—
And in the Spring! the spring!
When the stars sing—

And in the spring! the spring!
When the stars sing—

138

The world's love stirs you first
To wild sweet thirst,
Mad combat glorious, and so
To what you know
Of love in living. Yes, to you first came
The joy past name
Of interchange—the small mouth pressed
To the warm breast!

But O the human brothers! We can feel
All, all below
These small ones know—
Earth fair and good,
The bubbling flood
Of life a-growing—in us multiplied
As man spreads wide;
Not into leaves alone,
Nor flesh and bone,
But roof and wall and wheel
Of stone and steel;
Soft foliage and gorgeous bloom
Of murmuring loom;
And fruit of joy—o'erburdened heart
Poured forth in art!
We can not only leap in the sun,
Wrestle and run,
But know the music-measured beat
Of dancing feet,
The interplay of hands—we hold
Delight of doing, myriad-fold.
Joy of the rose we know—
To bloom—to grow;
Joy of the beast we prove
To strive—to move;
And in the spring! the spring!
When the stars sing—
Wide gladness of all living men
Comes back again.
A conscious universe at rest
In one's own breast!
The world's love! Wholly ours,
Through the breathing flowers,
Through all the living tumult of the wood

In us made good,
Through centuries that rise and fall—
We hold it all!
The world's love! Given words at last to speak,
Though yet so weak.
The world's love! Given hands that hold so much—
Lips that may touch—
The world's love! Sweet—it lies
In your dear eyes!

In Alabama Woods

The wet, dark woods—monotonous tall pines,
The heavy velvet mat of brown below,
And straight shafts rising, sodden black with rain,
In clean, long lines.

From stem to stem, a high-hung solemn pall,
Thick clouds of blue-green needles cover all;
But see, across the gloom, again! again!
The dogwood's flame of snow!

The Sphynx of Stone

In the calmness of graven stone—
Graven without
By the forces that carve the world.
Hardened within
By the hardness born of negation—
By the intricate contradiction
Of every line of advance,

She waits—she has waited long.
Many have come and guessed
And the only answer is death.
Many have never dared—
And most of all pass by
Seeing no riddle there.

A sphynx with a riddle old—
A sphynx of graven stone.
Calm are the quiet eyes
Calm is the quiet mouth
Calm is the breast of stone.
And the great limbs of the breast
Are still as the hills at night.

To Isadora Duncan

I have seen ballets. Hard-legged women
Hopping on stiffly distorted ugly foot-pegs;
Spinning like toy tops; whirling senseless petticoats,
Short and conventional, graceless as powder-puffs,
With the hard legs thrusting forth from the center.

* * *

I have seen Isadora. I have seen dancing.
She, loving, motherly, utterly gracious,
Grave in her suave folded robes; and around her
Blossomed the maidens, budded the children.
Lovely young maids with their light limbs leaping,
Arms tossing wide in the grace of young gladness,
Joy in their movement, joy in their faces.

I have seen dancing; soft-footed music;
Free naked feet, with each step a caressing,
White knees uplifting, white arms outwaving,
Fair growing maids and the fairy wee children,
Light as the flowers are, light as the snow-flake.
Leaping as the heart leaps—Springtime! Morning!

All blossom free from the heart of Isadora,
Mother of music, of melody in motion;
She, recreator of long-vanished wonder,
Mother of happiness! Mother of beauty!

RIVER WINDOWS

The Frame

Sky windows high over the Hudson,
    Wide wonder of water and light;
High windows, wide on the sunset,
    Wide windows, black on the night.

Blending

Sometimes that long, high-lying western wall
Grays up into a bank of evening cloud,
Blending and dim; vague river to vague sky;
Only pricked lights—too regular for stars—
To show the margin between earth and heaven.

Barges

Slow barges, loaded high and wide,
    With rose-red tiles;
Low barges, weighted to the tide
    With broken blue-stone piles;
Broad barges, full from side to side
    With gold-brown earth a-heap;
        Come sweeping down in light and pride,
        Go creeping up when light has died,
In chains of stars asleep.

Colors

From coral dawn to twilight jade
    The great sky jewel turns and glows;
        Saphire and light—
        Saphire at night—
Saphire and gold and rose.

A ribbon of green the thin park winds,
    By azure water, winding, too;
        A ribbon of grass—
        A ribbon of glass—
A ribbon of green and blue.

Children under the May-leaved trees,
Flying flowers of the park are they.
    Lilac and cream—
    Lilac and green—
Lilac and rose and gray.

A Cold Day

Purple, ruffled purple, when the wind blows up the blue,
Fringed and frosted with the white-caps as they run;
    Broken ice, dull gray and white
    In the hard wind-sharpened light,
And the staring cliffs across there, bald and dun.

Afternoon

A gray-blue sheet of rippled silk
    The wide, still river lies,
Slow-flowing, snowy plumes of steam
Melt like a disappearing dream
    Into the drowsy skies.

Far pants the fleeting motor-boat;
    Far puffs the crawling train.
Smoothly the distant tug-boats go,
With sail-furled schooners, stately, slow,
    Or barges long in chain.

Good Cheer

Going gaily down the stream;
Flagged with forward-flying steam,
    Brisk and red the tug-boats run;
Twinkling blue the river's flow,
Bank and border crisp with snow,
    All ablaze with morning sun.

My Clouds

As those who live on mountains see the clouds
Stealing below them in the valleys green,
Rising around them, billowing and soft;
We, in our cliff-side dwellings, watch the steam

143

From river-bordering trains,—a drifting plume,
That rolls among the poplars, tumbling white
Against the slopes of green, the river's blue;
And rising, white and glorious in the sun,
Whirling, on-rushing, up and up it pours—
Charging upon our windows in the clouds.

Blue and White

Blue and white! Blue and white!
   The river's full of ice.
Driving with the current and the tide,
   Riding swiftly, crowding low,
   In the strong mid-river flow—
Sliding softly, crushing slowly, up the side.

Blue and white! Blue and white!
   The sky is full of clouds;
Shining in the splendor of the sun;
   Flying wide and wild away
   Through the short, wind-ridden day—
Grouping softly, crowding closely, when it's done.

Steam

Tall by the tree-walled towering cliffs, all snow,
Remote, remote and dim, the mills across;
Glassed in still water; their vague shimmering towers
Marred by slow drift of loose, snow-crusted ice.

Snow-mist and river-fog and mingling steam;
Wreaths from the distant chimneys rising slow;
Long streaming plumes from busy tugs below,
Puffs from the panting derrick engine near,
And volleying clouds from each long laboring train.

Sunset on Riverside

Watching the gold light flush to rose,
   The rose light dull to gray,
     And the gray light dim
     Till the farther brim
   Dies out with the dying day.

Then the silver stars shine out above,
　　And the gold stars shine below;
　　　Their long stems shiver
　　　In the glassy river
　　Like flame flowers standing so.

And smooth across the glimmering field
　　Vague vessels bear at ease
　　　Their trailing flights
　　　Of clustered lights,
　　Like captive Pleiades.

White Days

Days when the shifting snow shuts off the sky;
Shuts off the distant shore, the mile of stream;
Blankets the anchored barges white and deep;
The slow, flat fields of floating shifting ice;
Sheets the deserted wharf in silent sleep;
Even the river white with drifting ice,
The slow, flat fields of floating shifting ice;
And, white as wool, outpouring, soft and high,
Whirling and changing as it billows by—
White rolls the flying steam.

River Lights

As black as ink, as smooth as oil,
　　In the long warm summer nights,
The river mirrors glassily
　　A double world of lights.

In shining rank on either bank
　　Clear lights the shores define;
Thick-starred they rise against the skies
　　Where fainter stars may shine.

And all along the water way
　　In gold and red and green,
Beauty and safety ride at peace,
　　Or pass in peace between.

Slow steamboats heavily loaded
　　With music and light and love,

The lamp-lit banks behind them,
　The starlit skies above.

They pass with a rushing murmur,
　Crested with gems they burn,
Dripping with light from the gunwale,
　Valenced from stem to stern.

They pass like moving islands
　Whose trees are a blazing pyre,
With roots that trail below them
　In a long thick fringe of fire.

My Pleasure Boats

Where treetops wave in level light when morning sunbeams glance,
　And river ripples run, all blue and bridling,
Magnolia-white the pleasure boats moored in the shallows dance,
　A flock of snowy ducks, so lightly sidling.

The twilight water welters bare, milk-blue and shining wide;
　Low smouldering sunset clouds beyond it hover,
Like shapeless logs the pleasure boats lie black along the tide,
　Till darkness falls at last to cool and cover.

Then every little pleasure boat sets out a starry light,
　On slim reflected limbs they stand and shiver,
Like a flock of little candles out playing in the night,
　Like little wading candles in the river.

OUT OF DOORS

Just to be out of doors! So still! So green!
With unbreathed air, illimitable, clean,
With soft, sweet scent of happy growing things,
The leaves' soft flutter, sound of sudden wings,
The far faint hills, the water wide between.

Breast of the great earth-mother! Here we lean
With no conventions hard to intervene,

146

Content, with the contentment nature brings,
  Just to be out of doors.

And under all the feeling half foreseen
Of what this lovely world will come to mean
To all of us when the uncounted strings
Are keyed aright, and one clear music rings,
In all our hearts. Joy universal, keen,
  Just to be out of doors.

WHERE SHADOW LIES

Under dull skies the paper lies
  Waiting my brain's command,
When sudden, on the empty sheet
The unveiled sunshine draws complete
  The shadow of my hand.

And by that shadow I am told
  Of newborn light behind,
That rainwashed skies in sunshine glow
And my glad pen the blaze can throw
  To those who still are blind.

Wait—can it be the shadow
  That shows the sunshine more?
Nay—'twas the light that proved the light—
The shadow gave no such delight,
  For that was there before!

And did no shadow of myself
  Obscure the paper fair
It still would speak to every one
In its clear answer to the sun
  Of the glory that is there!

THE SANDS

It runs—it runs—the hourglass turning,
Dark sands glooming, bright sands burning,

I turn, and turn, with heavy or hopeful hands,
So must I turn as long as the Voice commands,
But I lose all count of the hours in watching the sliding sands.

Or fast, or slow, it ceases turning,
Ceases the flow, or bright or burning—
"What have you done with the hours?" the voice demands;
What can I say of eager or careless hands?
I had forgotten the hours in watching the sliding sands.

No Summer

To those who in leisure may meet
    Comes Summer, green, fragrant and fair,
    With roses and stars in her hair,
Summer, as motherhood sweet—
    To us, in the waste of the street
    No Summer, only—The Heat.

To those of the fortunate fold
    Comes Winter, snow-clean and ice-bright,
    With joy for the day and night,
Winter, as fatherhood bold—
    To us, without silver or gold,
    No Winter,—only—The Cold.

In Twilight Park

In Twilight Park one never sees—
An hour of sun, because the trees—
    Stretch out so thick, stretch up so high,
    They cover almost all the sky,
Backed by the mountain's huddled knees.

It's a good place for eye-disease
Or hoarding gloomy memories,
    Sitting all dolorous and shy,
    Under grey ledges never dry
    In Twilight Park.

There is a damp distressful breeze
A murmur of rheumatic bees,
   And in deep chasms far & nigh
   Long waterfalls forever cry—
O come and take your summer ease
   In Twilight Park!

ON A TUB OF BUTTER, CHRISTMAS 1882

Most true and tender friend!
  You called your gift
Utilitarian; and seemed to think
That poetry and sentiment were lost
Because of common everyday delight
And hourly usefulness of such a thing.
Now let me show you that
The thought was wrong.
You should have seen my mother lift the cloth
That hid the glowing luxury below!
A breath of such deep fragrance rose as brought
To mind wide visions of past country life:
The airy kitchen with the open door
And feeding hens outside: the shining pans
And milkpails drying in the summer sun:
The worn old barn, with curving roof and low
Dark doorway where the cows come trooping in
And crowd with clumsy patience to their stalls.
The long green lane with the wild cherry trees
Where in unlucky summers the white nests
Of caterpillars spoiled the tender green.
The whole wide country road, down which the cows
Were driven day by day.
Its deep worn ruts, and strips of ragged turf on either side,
The low stone wall surmounted by a fence
Of ragged rails and tangle of long vines.
And the wide pasture, where the sun lies hot,
And all the cattle gather in the shade
Of arching trees; or stand in still content
And let the water ripple round their sides.
A little river. But the banks were green;
And it ran in and out among the fields

And had deep holes where stealthy pickerel hid,
And shallows that a child might run across;
Where blue-spired flowers grew rank,
And dragon flies
Danced with bright wings like bits of flying heat.

Now surely you will see
That thoughts like these
Are far from unpoetical;
Yet these
Came all from your utilitarian gift.

I need not say I thank you: that you know.

To Mary Shaw On Her Birthday, 1922.

Dear Mary Shaw! No name more dear
On all the modern stage we hear!
  Great woman! Standing with the few
  Who see the truth, who hail the new,
True artist, mother, friend and seer!

Strong in your art you still appear,
Strong in your heart you draw us near,
  Your heart and brain have held us true,
    Dear Mary Shaw.

We come because you bring us here,
Because you've helped us many a year,
  Because of love and honor due,
  Because we're all so fond of you,
    Dear Mary Shaw!

For A Guest Book

A house on a hillside set
  By the blue and silver river,
No city noise and fret

In the house on a hillside set—
Here you may care forget—
   Here is the comfort-giver,
In her house on a hillside set.
   By the blue and silver river.

A book for the grateful guest
   Go give thanks for beauty & pleasure,
To write of fair peace & rest—
In the book for the grateful guest,
And the joys by each held best,
   Of friendship, ease and leisure,
A book for the grateful guest
   To give thanks for beauty & pleasure.

LECTURE VERSE [NO. 1]

To all you friends who've gathered here tonight,
   And paid for this address with solid money,
I want to say—don't look for wild delight—
   This lecture isn't funny!

It is an earnest lecture, written straight
   From out one woman's heart to enter many;
And if you ask excuse for facts, I state—
   Alas! I haven't any!

For facts are stubborn things, and it is true,
   In spite of chivalry and poem and story,
That so far, in the race of which are you—
   Man has the glory.

The glory and the shame! He did the deeds
   Which fill the world with beauty, power, and wonder;
He kept supplied the wider human needs,—
   And kept us under!

And what I wish to urge, to thinking minds,
   Is that the race will thrive, both man and woman,
When every baby in its parents find,
   That *both* are Human!

151

Fair Friends, in opening lectures like to these,
    With hope to please
Yet teach the heart to swell, the brain to climb
    At the same time;
I feel I must when first I meet your eyes apologize.

For this is not a field where thought can soar
    As heretofore
And things sublime or things ridiculous
    Each one discuss
While all the little listening girls and boys
    "Huer the great noise!"

I offer you today in place of this
    Discursive bliss
A field of solemn facts, with some pretense
    Of Inference!
In place of thought and fancy soaring free—
    Biography!

Alas! Biography is solid work one cannot shirk!
Facts about lives that are with history blent
    I can't invent,
Must serve in place of warmest disputation
Chill facts—a cold *collation*.

MER-SONGS

1. The Mer-Baby

We all have heard of mermaids,
With hair so rich and long,
And a comb of gold and a glass to hold,
And soft seductive song.

But how could mermaids ever live,
Big mermaids fair and free,
Without a year of that small dear,
The little mer-babie?

152

The mer-babies are soft and sweet,
And smooth and fat and fair,
With dots of scales on their little tales,
And shiny streaks of hair.

The mer-babies have beds of foam
In the cradles of the deep;
And waves lap slow and winds breathe low
When the wee mer-babies sleep.

The mer-babies are always clean;
They swim and crawl and climb;
And dig and play in the sea-sand grey,—
But they're bathing all the time!

They cut their teeth on coral, of course,
They eat from pearly shells,—
O happy and free in the shining sea
The wee mer-baby dwells.

2. The Mer-Dolly.

The little mer-baby she had a mer-doll,
   A little mer-doll-dolly!
She loved it dearly, she did indeed,
And dressed it gaily in bright sea-weed,
   As fine as a parrot polly.

The mer-dolly's teeth they were tiny pearls,
   Her lips were of coral merely,
Her cheeks were little sea-shells pink,
And she could talk but she couldn't think—
   At least she couldn't think clearly!

The little mer-doll had a crown of gold—
   That little mer-doll-dolly!
The little mer-babies sat at her feet,
The little mer-girls said, "isn't she sweet!"
   And the little mer-boys said, "jolly!"

3. The Mer-Baby and the Land-Baby

The little land-baby she sat on the land,
   The mer-baby sat on the sea,

The little land-baby was dusty with sand,
And the mer-baby, on the other hand,
    Was as wet as wet could be!

The little land-baby was thoroughly dressed
    From her shoes to her well-brushed hair;
She had ribbons and ruffles and all the rest,
And delicate petticoats starched and pressed,
    But the little mer-baby was bare!

The little land-baby she mustn't do this,
    And alas she mustn't do that!
She had care and comfort and many a kiss,
But she was as thin as a "hankerfiss,"
    And the little mer-baby was fat!

The landbaby's nurse came and carried her home,
    Away from the shining sea;
But the little mer-baby could wriggle and roam
And frolic and splash in the soft seam foam—
    Now which would you rather be?

4. The Little Mer-Girls

Said the little mer-girls to the big mermaid
"We want to be big like you!
With longer tails, and shinier scales,
And hair more wavy and blue!"

Said the little mer-girls to the big mermaid,
"We want to have golden combs!"
And waver and swing and float and sing,
Where the shore-wave breaks and foams!"

Said the little mer-girls to the big mermaid,
"We want to have mirrors too!
And sing to the sailors, the fishers and whalers,
And carry them down like you!"

Said the big mermaid to the little mer-girls,
"O dear little sisters—be young!
For we weary of foam, of glass and of comb,

154

And the sailors are drowned when we carry them
    home—
When the songs are over and sung!"

5. Running Away to Land

I will tell you now a story
Which I think you'll understand,
About a little mer-boy
That ran away to land.

He ran away to land he did,
From out the shining sea,
For he wanted to be wandering—
He wanted to be free!

And all the mer-child fairy-books
Are full of wondrous tales,
Of a land of snowy mountain-peaks,
A land of grassy vales,

A land where birds are musical,
A land where flowers are sweet,
Where everybody has two tails,
And calls them legs and feet!

He ran away to land he did,
One midnight cold and black,
But he found he could not walk at all—
And so he came right back!

6. The Quarrel

There was once an awful quarrel—
As fierce as fierce could be
Between a land-boy on the land,
And a mer-boy on the sea.

Said the land-boy to the mer-boy,
"I wouldn't have a tail like you!"
Said the mer-boy to the land-boy,
"I wouldn't be split in two!"

Said the land-boy to the mer-boy,
"I can run and jump and climb,
And I can dive and swim besides—
But you swim all the time!"

Said the mer-boy to the land-boy,
"You can only breathe in air,—
And you drown beneath the water,
But I breath everywhere!"

"On the land you just move sideways,
Sticking to earth so brown—
In the water, blue and lovely,
"I can travel *up and down!*"

Then the land-boy pelted him with dirt—
A thing a mer-boy loathes;
So he ducked the land-boy in the surf,
And spoiled his Sunday clothes."

7. Mer-Play

Where the beach is flat and flowing,
   Wavelets coming, wavelets going,
   There the small Mer-children play,
   In silver night, in golden day,—
   They need never go away.

As we love the sight of ocean,
Sound and color, light and motion,
   All mer-children, understand,
   Love the stretches of warm sand—
   Dearly love to play on land.

As each earth-born son and daughter
Loves the feeling of the water,
   Rippling, rolling, here and there,
   Over small feet brown and bare—
   So the Mer-child loves the air.

Large ones catch the tails of small ones,
Little ones trip up the tall ones,
   Diving swiftly out of reach,

Laughing gaily each to each,
Playing on the breezy beach.

8. *Mer-Pleasures*

Of all the pleasures that Mer-children meet
    These two are the very best—
They never are scolded for wetting their feet,
    They never are washed and dressed.
    The scolding fails
        When feet are tails.
    And tails
        Have scales;
    Bathing is best
        When done
        At rest
        Undressed.

If they wish to be dry they can sit in the sun,
    On warm brown rocks, at ease;
But the little Mer-children every one
    Keep close to the slippery seas.
    They love to be
        All wet and free,
        Like thee,
    And me;
    They have no care
        Of things to wear,
    All bare
    And fair.

If they stayed too long on the sunny shore,
    Forgetting the waters nigh,
They might have a scolding—or something more—
    For letting their tails get dry!
    From Mer-Mama,
        Or stern Mer-Pa—
        Ah-ha!
        La-la!
    Mer-children know,
        And never go
        Dry so—
        Oh no!

9. Mer-Swimming

Bright little scales all lapping, lapping,
  In shining row on row;
Tight little tails all flapping, flapping,
  Swift-flapping to and fro.

Sometimes they swim with arms abroad,
  Sometimes with folded hands,
Sometimes as swift as a whirling sword,
  Then slow as sinking sands.

Up through the waters lifting, lifting,
  Waters of lightening blue;
Down through the waters, shifting, shifting,
  Slow-shifting down and through.

Sometimes they swim like a rising spark,
  Sometimes they drop like lead,
Sometimes they float like the Spanish bark,
  Then sink to the ocean's bed.

Glittering scales all gleaming, gleaming,
  Through waters green and dim,
Flittering tails all streaming, streaming,
  Where the gay Mer-children swim.

10. Mer-Playthings

If you were a merry Mer-boy
  Beneath the rolling tide,
If you had been good, and better than good,
And had a Mer-Father who could—and would—
  He *might* give you a sea-horse to ride!
    You could charge with the breakers
    And fly with the foam,
    And roll with the rollers,
    And never go home
  Till you ached in your mer-inside.

If you were a slender Mer-girl,
  Below the shimmering wet,
If you had been good, and better than good,

158

And a Mer-mother who could and would—
  She *might* give you a sea-puss to pet!
    A soft sea-pussy to curl and purr,
    On you would be ever so fond of her,
    And her sly little tricks forget.

If you were a Mer-child,
  Baby or grown quite old,
If you had been good and better than good,
And had Mer-parents who could—and would—
  They *might* give you a galleon's gold!
    Golden playthings to roll and throw,
    To build gold houses and lay them low,
    Easy and smooth to hold.

11. The Mermaid's Search

A mermaid went a-searching,
  For her heart was empty and cold;
She was tired of her combs and mirrors,
  She was tired of her pearls and gold.

She was tired of the creaming breakers,
  She was tired of laughter and song,
She was tired of luring sailors,
  Who never loved her long.

She searched in the sandy shallows,
  And found, day after day,
Only the bones of sailors—
  Poor sailors thrown away.

She searched in the deep green hollows,
  And what do you think she found?
Only a little baby—
  A baby that was drowned.

She pressed it close to her bosom
  Under her long hair's veil;
She kissed it and hugged it and rocked it,
  As she swayed on her long green tail.

She was young with immortal beauty,
  She was old as the sea is old—

But the baby could never kiss her,
  And her heart was empty and cold.

12. The Mer-Menagerie

An old Mer-man he took his Mer-wife,
  And their Mer-children small,
Over long sea-miles, on the soft sea-grass,
  To the park with the high sea-wall
Sea-girdles wore they, and sea-garlands gay,
  By the green sea-willows tall.

They stand with the crowds all laughing,
  Where the sea-apes mop and mow,
They go round on the swift sea-horses—
  A Triton showed them how;
They find a sea-cat, sea-mouse, sea-rat,
  Sea-hog, sea-calf, sea-cow.

They ride the great sea-elephant,
  Hear the sea-lions roar,
Sea-leopards and sea-panthers growl
  Behind the grated door,
Sea-wolf, sea-bear, sea-fox, sea-hare,
  Sea-porcupines galore.

They watch the sea-birds resting
  On their sea-perches low,
The sea-lark and sea-swallow,
  Sea-robin and sea-crow,
Sea-eagle and sea-pheasant,
  With the sea-owl blinking so.

By the cages of sea-monsters
  The small sea-urchins quail,
At the sting of the sea-scorpion,
  And the great sea-dragon's tail,
Sea-spider and sea-serpent,
  Sea-toad, sea-slug, sea-snail.

But the little Mer-girls wander
  On the sea-moss waving free,
Their hands they fill with sea-daffodil

And sea-anemone,
Sea-pink, sea-heath and sea-holly,
And the sea-ferns greenery.

They picnic on sea-cucumbers,
Hardboiled sea-eggs (though high,)
Sea-cabbage and sea-onion,
Sea-pudding and sea-pie,
Sea-grapes and pink sea-lemonade—
Can Mer-folks throats be dry?

Maybe you are doubtful, very, of sea-beasts such a score,
But if you look in the dictionary, you'll find them all, and more.

THE BAD LITTLE COO-BIRD

In the morning, in the bed,
She hugged her baby close and said,
"You're my little coo-bird, and this is our nest—
"My little Coo-bird, that I love the best—
"Now coo! little coo-bird, coo!"
And what did that bad baby do?
"Coo," said the mother soft and still—
Piped little daughter loud and shrill—
"Cock-a-doodle-doo!"

"No! no!" said the mother, "no!"
I do not like it so!
I want no cock-a-biddys in my bed!"
And she brooded her nestling warm and said,
"Now coo! little coo-bird, coo!"
And what did that bad baby do?
"Coo," said the mother soft and still—
Piped little daughter loud and shrill—
"To-whoo! To-whit!—to-whoo!"

"No! no!" said the mother, "no!"
I do not like it so!
Such fowls as owls I do not love—
Where is my little cooing dove?
"Now coo! little coo-bird, coo!"

And what did that dear baby do?
"Coo," said the mother soft and slow—
Laughed little daughter sweet and low—
"Coo! Coo-oo! Coo!"

The Little Digger

A little brown gnome went a-digging in the ground,
  Digging deeply, digging downy;
And what do you think that little digger found?
  The little elf!—the little brownie!

First came the grass with the dewy leaves and shoots,
  Green and wavy, green and pearly;
Then came the network of hungry little roots,
  White and eager, white and curly.

Then came the mould and the sand and the clay,
  Brown and grayish, red and yellow;
Then the hard stones that are always in the way
  Of a scratching little fellow.

Then the great rocks with the shining streaks of gold,
  And the silver, and the copper;
And he filled his little pockets as full as they could hold,
  As a miller fills a hopper.

And then the great caves where the jewels are the light,
  Jewels glancing, jewels gleaming;
With stalactites and stalagmites and the water dripping bright;
  —Like a dream when you are dreaming.

He dug to look for loveliness, and loveliness he found,
  Digging deeply, digging downy,
There is beauty in the air and sea and beauty in the
    ground—
  No one knows it but the Brownie!

THE LITTLE PRINCESSES

There was once a King and a Queen
In a land you never have seen,
  Their little Princesses
  Wore golden dresses,
And danced in a garden green!

The little Princesses were three,
As fair as fair could be,
  Their hair was gold and their eyes were blue,
  And they each had a crown and a sceptre too,
And a throne of ivory!

Their pillows were soft 'tis said,
But they never were sent to bed,
  They played all night
  In the silver light,
And slept in the morning red!

Their slippers had silver soles,
Their milk was in golden bowls,
  And butter and sugar and jelly so red
  They mixed and stirred and sprinkled and spread,
All over their breakfast rolls!

A WALK, WALK, WALK

I once went out for a walk, walk, walk,
  For a walk beside the sea;
And all I carried to eat, eat, eat
Was a jar of ginger-snaps so sweet,
  And a jug of ginger tea.

For I am fond of cinnamon pie,
  And peppermint puddings too,
And I dearly love to make, make, make,
A mighty mass of mustard cake,
  And nutmeg beer to brew.

163

And all I carried to drink, drink, drink,
  That long and weary way,
Was a dozen little glasses
Of boiled molasses
  On a Cochin China tray.

For I am fond of the sugar of the grape,
  And the sugar of the maple tree,
But I always eat
the sugar of the beet
  When I'm in company.

And all I carried to read, read, read,
  For a half an hour or so,
Was the works of Dumas, Pere et fils,
And Milman's Rome, and Grote on Greece,
  And the poems of Longfellow.

For I am fond of Hunting the Snark,
And the Romaunt of the Rose,
And I never go to bed
Without Webster at my head,
And Worcester at my toes.

AUNT ELIZA

Seven days had Aunt Eliza
Read the Boston Advertiser,
    Seven days on end;
But in spite of her persistance
Still she met with some resistance
    From her bosom friend.

Thomas Brown, the Undertaker
Who declared he'd have to shake her,
    Daily called at ten;
Asking if dear Aunt's condition
Would allow of his admission,
    With his corps of men.

Aunt Eliza heard him pleading,
Ceased an instant from her reading,
    Softly downward stole;
Soon broke up the conversation,
Punctuating Brown's oration,
    With a shower of coal.

CHILLY WEATHER

A merry little monkey met a sorry little ápe,
    In the edges of the sedges by the sea,
The one he wore a tippet and the other wore a cape,
And they both of them were cold as they could be.

Said the monkey "I am freezing
And I find it isn't pleasing,"
    But the other only answered with a moan;
Said the monkey, "Let's run faster
Till we find a mustard plaster,
    Or something that will warm us to the bone."

But the doleful ape suggested
That they get a little rested
    In the masses of the grasses by the sea,
So they laid them down together
In the chilly wintry weather,
    And they both were frozen stiff as they could be.

A DREAM OF GOLD

He sat alone, encumbered with his Gold
Alone beside the border of the lake,
And far across the water's shimmering bed
He saw a lady in a little boat,
A Lady lovely as a summer's dream,
Dreamed in the depths of mild full mooned night.

The lady waited till the middle night,
For she had fell designs upon his gold,

165

And meant to linger till he fell to dream,
Sleeping beside the border of the lake;
And then she planned to leave the little boat
And roll him down into a watery bed.

Little she recked of how that beauteous bed
Would claim her too, while the unhappy night
Looked down to see the drifting oarless boat,
The drifting moon-light on the piles of gold,
The drifting shadows on the level lake;
And all as vague and silent as a dream.

Soft stole she to him, noiseless as a dream,
But he rose up upon his glittering bed,
And sat there like a lily on a lake,
And asked her if she'd like to spend the night
In sitting there by him to count his gold
Better than floating broadcast in a boat.

She answered him that she preferred the boat,
And begged him not to interrupt her dream,
Stating that she had only thought of gold
When tossing wearily upon her bed,
In indigestive watches of the night,
There in her lonely bower beside the lake.

But he maintained she ought to like the lake,
And softly beckoned her into the boat,
And drowned her in the middle of the night,
And then returned to dimly drowse and dream
There on the margin in his shining bed,
All lit and glimmering with plenteous gold.

Envoy

Sweet is much gold and sweet a lovely lake,
Better a lady in her bed than boat,
And the best dreams are those that fly by night.

THE MELANCHOLY RABBIT

A melancholy rabbit, in distress,
    We heard complaining on the moonlit mead,

166

And neither we nor anyone could guess
   If he were ill at ease, or ill indeed.

We heard complaining on the moonlit mead,
   We sought the lonely wanderer to relieve;
If he were ill at ease or ill indeed,
   We did not ask—sufficient he should grieve.

We sought the lonely wanderer to relieve
   With sundry bundles of electric hay;
We did not ask—sufficient he should grieve—
   If he were used to dieting that way.

With sundry bundles of electric hay
   The suffering hare was speedily supplied;
If he were used to dieting that way
   It could be the reason that he died.

The suffering hare was speedily supplied—
   A melancholy rabbit in distress;
It could not be the reason that he died—
   And neither we nor anyone could guess.

A USE OF MEMORY

Why should I think of dragging clouds,
Of dreary, dragging clouds of grey,
When I have seen them floating light,
Snow-mountains blazing soft and bright,
Or filmy feathers faint and white,
   On many a bygone day?

Why should I think of sighing winds,
Of sighing winds that shake the rain,
When I've felt breezes fresh and clear
That sing forever past my ear,
And breaths of summer drifting near
   O'er clover-fields and grain?

Why should I think of days like this,
Of days like this, all dark and wet,

167

When I've known days so grandly bright,
So full of freedom and delight,
That, though all after life were night,
    I never can forget?

MOTION

We all like motion. Why not grow to feel
Smooth-rolling Time beneath us, and enjoy
The steady, quiet, ceaseless flow of years;
The whirr of flying seconds; the swift beat
Of minutes as they pass; the beaded days,
Thick-starred with Sundays regular and swift;
The moon-set months, fast wheeling up the sky;
The seasons opening and closing calm,
Year after year in long processional;
Even to feel the heaving centuries
Wheel on beneath us, slow, but moving still?

CLOSED DOORS

When it is night and the house is still,
    When it is day and guests are gone,
When the lights and colors and sounds that fill
    Leave the house empty and you alone:

Then you hear them stir—you hear them shift—
    You hear them through the walls and floors—
And the door-knobs turn and the latches lift
    On the closet doors.

Then you try to read and you try to think,
    And you try to work—but the hour is late;
No play nor labor nor meat nor drink
    Will make them wait.

Well for you if the locks are good!
    Well for you if the bolts are strong,

And the panels heavy with oaken wood,
   And the chamber long.

Even so you can hear them plead—
   Hear them argue—hear them moan—
When the house is very still indeed,
   And you are alone.

Blessed then is a step outside,
   Warm hands to hold you, eyes that smile,
The stir and noise of a world that's wide,
   To silence yours for a little while.

Fill your life with work and play!
   Fill you heart with joy and pain!
Hold your friends while they will stay,
   Silent so shall these remain.

But you can hear them when you hark—
   Things you wish you had not known—
When the house is very still and dark,
   And you are alone.

[THE GREEN SLOPES CREAM WITH 'INNOCENTS' SNOW]

The green slopes cream with 'innocents' snow,
   The woods are warm with Spring,
   Mile after mile
   White fear-blooms smile;
     And then,
      Again,
   As the train whirls swift
   'Round the hills' green lift—
Pink peach-trees suddenly sing!

LITTLE FLUTTERS OF CALIFORNIA BEAUTY

   In the vast velvet garden,
   In the wide soft rolling garden,

169

In the golden gleaming garden
Of our California green.

Where the wild flowers crowd to your knee, to your knee,
And the tame flowers arch overhead . . .

Where the mile-wide orchards of red-tipped trees
Make hazy floors of brown . . .

Along the reeling wheeling aisles
Of level vineyards, miles on miles . . .

Long lines of eucalyptus run, an endless race, an easy grace,
Free verse in living green.

THE GRAPEVINE

To a Paradise world of flowers—
    By a way that was long and winding—
Cold and windy the hours—
To a Paradise world of flowers—
From the dark where the mountain towers—
    To a beauty bright and blinding
To a Paradise world of flowers—
    By a way that was long & winding.

SANTA BARBARA TO SAN JOSE

I came from Santa Barbara—
I went to San Jose—
Blue sky above—blue sea beside,
Wild gold along the way—
The lovely lavish mustard gold
Ran wild along the way.

The purple mountains loomed beyond,
The soft hills rolled between,
From crest to crest,
Like smoke at rest,
The eucalyptus screen
Its careless foliage drifting by
Against that blue enfolding sky
In wreaths of dusky green—
With drowsing live-oak masses thick
On the slopes of April green—
More joy than any eye can hold—
In restful blue, in rousing gold—
Bright bronze & olive green.

CALIFORNIA COLORS

A Song.

I came from Santa Barbara,
I went to San Jose,
Blue sky above—blue sea beside,
Wild gold along the way—
The lovely lavish blossom gold
Ran wild along the way.

The purple mountains loomed beyond,
The soft hills rolled between,
From crest to crest, like smoke at rest,
The eucalyptus screen
Its careless foliage drifting by
Against that all-enfolding sky
In dusky glimmering green;
With live-oak masses drowsing dark
On the slopes of April green;
More joy than any eye can hold,
Not only blue, not only gold,
But bronze and olive green.

Appendix

The following list, dated 12 February 1935, was prepared by Gilman for Amy Wellington and indicates those poems that were intended for inclusion in this edition. I have eliminated duplicate titles, corrected misnumbering, added explanatory information in brackets, where appropriate, and appended to the end of the list additional poems mentioned in correspondence that Gilman was apparently considering for inclusion in the volume. Gilman wrote the words "unassorted list" at the top of the first page; the list does not reflect the order in which she intended the poems to appear.

1. Some Nordics
2. Happiness
3. Hyenas
4. A Psalm of "Lives"
5. The Gunman
6. Group: River Windows, 14 of 'em
7. The Oyster and the Starfish
8. Religious Toleration
9. The Powdered Nose. 4 of 'em [only one poem with this title was found in the folder.]
10. Twigs
11. The Front Wave
12. The Pious Pawn
13. Just to be Out of Doors
14. The Departing Housemaid
15. The Son of Both
16. The Fatalist and the Sailorman
17. Why? To The United States of America 1915–16
18. To Isadora Duncan
19. Our World "Is it so hard"
20. The Kingdom
21. The Earth, the World & I
22. Two Prayers
23. Our World. International Hymn
24. More Females of The Species
25. The Flag of Peace
26. A Social Puzzle
27. An Army With Banners
28. Song for The World's Flag

29. The Real Religion
30. There Are Those Who Can See
31. Begin Now
32. This is The Year
33. Queer People
34. "I Would Fain die a dry death!"
35. High Sovereignty
36. This is a Lady's Hat. A trio of triolets
37. A Diet Undesired
38. The Speaker's Sin
39. Child Labor [Two different versions appear in the folder of poems.]
40. The Cripple
41. Thankfulness
42. The New "Youth"—Neither Youth Nor Age
43. Mrs. Noah
44. The Internationalist
45. The War-Skunk
46. The Lord of Strife
47. The Love of Human Kind
48. Pikers
49. The Bitten Grass
50. The Santa Claus Story
51. Where Shadow Lies
52. Another Creed
53. Why Nature Laughs
54. The Weeping Nautilus
55. We Eat at Home
56. The Rabbit, The Rhinoceros & I
57. To Mothers
58. Whatever Is
59. Santa Barbara to San Jose
60. Ode to the Cook
61. Kitchen Women
62. The Human Law
63. To The Indifferent Women (Sestina)
64. A Use of Memory
65. Matriatism
66. The Housewife
67. The Central Sun
68. The Sands
69. No Summer
70. The Queen
71. Up & Down
72. Limiting Life
73. Thoughts & Facts
74. The Primal Power

75. The Purpose
76. Noblesse Oblige
77. Parent & Child
78. The Source
79. The Coming Day
80. The Fool Killer
81. Little Leafy Brothers
82. Mer-Babies & the other child verses [The "other" child verses include six additional poems not identified separately on Gilman's list.]
83. Patient Truth
84. From Two Albums
85. On a Tub of Butter
86. To the Packer
87. How about the Man!
88. The Packer's Hand
89. To Mary Shaw
90. The Day of Freedom. Chant Royal.
91. Still With Us. 1910
92. The Tree & The Sun
93. The Women of 1920
94. We and Honduras
95. Lecture verses
96. " "
97. The Daily Squid
98. My View
99. Hats & Base Ball
100. On Germany
101. Where Women Meet
102. A Vandal
103. "Special Dry Toast"
104. Dixie [This poem was titled "Happy Day" in manuscript. There was, however, a note appended to the poem stating that it was written to the tune of "Dixie."
105. Good Will
106. Cal[ifornia]. "flutters"
107. To Poverty
108. The Melting Pot
109. State Sovereignty
110. One Girl of Many
111. Body of Mine
112. The Yellow Reporter
113. Two Callings
114. For a Guestbook
115. In Twilight Park
116. Motion
117. I am Human

118. The Proposal (Rondeau)
119. A Protest
120. Full Motherhood
121. Between Past & Future
122. The Eternal Mother to the Bachelor Maid
123. This Lovely Earth

Following is a list of additional poems mentioned for inclusion in correspondence between Amy Wellington and Gilman:

1. Worship
2. Closed Doors
3. In Alabama Woods
4. California Colors
5. [The green slopes cream with 'innocents' snow]
6. The Sphynx of Stone
7. Aunt Eliza
8. The Melancholy Rabbit
9. Wings
10. The Artist
11. A Dream of Gold
12. The Grapevine
13. En Banc
14. Dark Ages

Notes

Introduction

1. Amy Wellington (1873–1948), Gilman's long-time friend, was a feminist author and former editor of *Current Opinion*. Wellington also contributed articles on feminist issues to the *Dial* in Chicago, the *New York Evening Post*, and the *Saturday Review of Literature*. Her best-known work was *Women Have Told: Studies in the Feminist Tradition* (Boston: Little, Brown, 1930). A clipping of Wellington's review of *The Living of Charlotte Perkins Gilman* is located in the papers of Lyman Beecher Stowe, Beecher Stowe Collection, Schlesinger Library, Radcliffe College, folder 414. Quoted by permission.

2. Gilman, *The Living of Charlotte Perkins Gilman*, (New York: Appleton-Century, 1935), 42–43. Hereafter, *Living*.

3. *New York Times*, 20 August 1936, 44.

4. Gilman ended her life by inhaling a lethal dose of chloroform.

5. Amy Wellington to Gilman dated 5 August 1935, folder 125, Gilman Papers, Schlesinger Library, Radcliffe College. Quoted by permission.

6. Gary Scharnhorst, "Reconstructing *Here Also*: On the Later Poetry of Charlotte Perkins Gilman," in *Critical Essays on Charlotte Perkins Gilman*, Joanne Karpinski, ed., (New York: G. K. Hall, 1992), 249–68.

7. Amy Wellington to Gilman, 5 August 1935, folder 125, Gilman Papers, Schlesinger Library, Radcliffe College. Quoted by permission.

8. Gilman to Lyman Beecher Stowe, 29 March 1935, folder 416, Beecher-Stowe Collection of Family Papers, Schlesinger Library, Radcliffe College.

9. Lyman Beecher Stowe to Gilman, 4 June 1935, folder 416, Beecher-Stowe Collection of Family Papers, Schlesinger Library, Radcliffe College.

10. Lyman Beecher Stowe to Gilman, 26 June 1935, folder 416, Beecher-Stowe Collection of Family Papers, Schlesinger Library, Radcliffe College.

11. Gilman to Lyman Beecher Stowe, 10 July 1935, folder 416, Beecher-Stowe Collection of Family Papers, Schlesinger Library, Radcliffe College.

12. Gilman to Lyman Beecher Stowe, 12 April 1935, folder 416, Beecher-Stowe Collection of Family Papers, Schlesinger Library, Radcliffe College.

13. Letter from Zona Gale to John L. B. Williams, Appleton-Century, 31 May 1935, folder 416, Beecher-Stowe Collection of Family Papers, Schlesinger Library, Radcliffe College. Gale remarked that she was "most enthusiastic" about the manuscript and would "especially like to write the introduction" because "no one had more influence [than Gilman] on [her] own thinking."

14. Gilman to Amy Wellington, 5 April 1935, folder 125, Gilman Papers, Schlesinger Library, Radcliffe College. Quoted by permission.

15. As early as 3 November 1933, Stowe betrayed mild annoyance in his response to Gilman's hint that he help her market "The Yellow Wall Paper" as a dramatic monologue. "Look here, I've had an idea!" Gilman wrote on 2 November. "Why, wouldn't

["The Yellow Wall Paper"] make a *gorgeous monologue!* Stage setting of the room *and the paper*, the four windows, the moonlight on the paper—changing lights and *movement*—and the woman staring! I could do it myself, in a drawing room and make everybody's flesh creep, but I think it would make a real Emperor Jones'y thing on the stage. . . . Perhaps Kate Hepburn would consider it—though she's pretty young. Oh, if [Alla] Nazimova would! She's not dead is she!? Maybe your august mama-in-law would know somebody—has she read it?" Stowe responded that although "The Yellow Wall Paper" "might make an excellent monologue," he knew "very little about such matters. . . . I am in the last mad rush on my Beecher book which is due the 15th of November for publication in February," he remarked. Stowe's summaries of his own work projects became a common theme in his letters to Gilman. See folder 416, Beecher-Stowe Collection of Family Papers, Schlesinger Library, Radcliffe College.

16. In various diary entries for 1922, Gilman reported that Wellington had been "hustle[d] off to Presbyterian Ho[spital]." where the doctors thought she might "linger four days or so" after performing the "worst operation they ever saw" for treatment of a "fibroid growth [that had] strangulated [her] intestine." Wellington, however, survived the surgery. See entries for 9 July, 15, 17, 19, and 20, 1922, in Vol. 2 of *The Diaries of Charlotte Perkins Gilman*, ed. Denise D. Knight, University Press of Virginia, 1994.

17. Amy Wellington to Gilman, 5 May 1935, folder 125, Gilman Papers, Schlesinger Library, Radcliffe College. Quoted by permission.

18. Ibid. Quoted by permission.

19. Amy Wellington to Gilman, 3 July 1935, folder 125, Gilman Papers, Schlesinger Library, Radcliffe College. Quoted by permission.

20. Amy Wellington to Gilman, 17 July 1935, folder 125, Gilman Papers, Schlesinger Library, Radcliffe College. Quoted by permission.

21. Gilman left only a small estate which was depleted within months after her death. There is no indication that Gilman acceded to Stowe's suggestion in his 4 June 1935, letter that "the contract with the publisher require the payment of one third of the royalties to Miss Wellington and the remaining two thirds to you or your heirs" (folder 416, Beecher-Stowe Collection of Family Papers, Schlesinger Library, Radcliffe College.) Without any promise of financial remuneration for her work, Wellington may have been disinclined to complete the edition.

22. Willis Kingsley Wing to Lyman Beecher Stowe, 29 August 1935, folder 420, Beecher-Stowe Collection of Family Papers, Schlesinger Library, Radcliffe College.

23. Katharine Beecher Stetson Chamberlin to Lyman Beecher Stowe, 15 July 1936, folder 417, Beecher-Stowe Collection of Family Papers, Schlesinger Library, Radcliffe College.

24. In size, this edition, which contains 167 poems, is slightly larger than Gilman's first volume of verse, *In This Our World*, which contained 149 poems in its longest edition.

25. "To D. G.," Gilman's tribute to dandelion greens, appeared in the 20 May 1880 issue of the *New England Journal of Education*. See Denise D. Knight, "Charlotte Perkins Gilman's Forgotten First Publication," in *ANQ: A Quarterly Journal of Short Articles, Notes, and Reviews*, 7.4 (October 1994): 223–25.

26. Gilman, "Feminism" (in typescript), folder 175, Gilman Papers, Schlesinger Library, Radcliffe College. Quoted by permission.

27. Cheryl Walker, ed. *American Women Poets of the Nineteenth Century: An Anthology*. (New Brunswick: Rutgers University Press, 1992), xxvi.

28. *Topeka State Journal*, 15 June 1896.

29. *Endure: The Diary of Charles Walter Stetson*, Mary A. Hill, ed. (Philadelphia: Temple University Press, 1985): 291.

30. Whitman's influence on Gilman's poetry was significant, particularly in her first volume of poetry. See Denise D. Knight, "'With the first grass-blade': Whitman's Influence on the Poetry of Charlotte Perkins Gilman," in *Walt Whitman Quarterly Review* (Summer 1993): 18–29.

31. Folder 165, Gilman Papers, Schlesinger Library, Radcliffe College. Quoted by permission.

32. Gilman, rev. of *Women and Labor* by Olive Schreiner, *Forerunner* 2 (July 1911): 197.

33. Gilman to Caroline Hill, 4 December 1921, folder 143, Gilman Papers, Schlesinger Library, Radcliffe College. Quoted by permission.

34. Floyd Dell, *Women as World Builders* (Chicago: Forbes, 1913): 24.

35. Traubel's review appeared in *Conservator* 9 (September 1898): 109.

36. Howells, "The New Poetry," *North American Review* 168 (May 1899): 589.

37. Ibid.

38. Howells, "Life and Letters," *Harper's Weekly* (25 January 1896): 79.

39. *Living*, 279–80.

40. Howells, "The New Poetry," *North American Review* 168 (May 1899): 590.

41. Gilman, lecture titled "Human Nature," presented to the Pasadena Nationalist Club, 15 June 1890, folder 163, Gilman Papers, Schlesinger Library, Radcliffe College. Quoted by permission.

42. Gilman was referring to the harsh criticism she had endured from those who branded her an unnatural mother after she relinquished custody of Katharine to Walter Stetson, following their divorce in 1894. Moreover, Gilman had enraged a number of people after she published a poem by Stetson's new wife, Grace Channing Stetson, in the *Impress*, a California literary weekly that she managed for several months in 1895. Channing and Gilman had been friends since 1879.

43. Gilman, "The New Motherhood," *Forerunner* 1 (December 1910): 17.

44. Wellington, "Charlotte Perkins Gilman," *Women Have Told: Studies in the Feminist Tradition*, (Boston: Little, Brown, 1930): 123.

45. Gilman, "The Artist," reprinted in this edition.

46. Gilman, "Human Nature," cf. note 41, above.

47. Gilman appended the remark, "California always makes me sing," on the manuscript copy of "Little flutters of California beauty."

48. The instructions appeared in Gilman's hand on the manuscript copy of the poem that was forwarded to Amy Wellington.

49. Gilman alludes to writing "The Bad Little Coo-Bird" in both her diary entry of 9 January 1891 and in her autobiography (*Living* 160–61).

50. Gilman, "The Dancing of Isadora Duncan," *Forerunner* 6 (April 1915): 101.

51. Numerous works by and about Gilman have been published in recent years. Readers wishing to have a fuller account of Gilman's life and literature should consult one or more of the works listed in the bibliography.

52. Amy Wellington to Gilman, 5 May 1935, folder 125, Gilman Papers, Schlesinger Library, Radcliffe College. Quoted by permission.

The Son of Both

Gilman added the notation, "[written] before 1910 I think." She signed the poem, Charlotte Perkins Stetson, however, suggesting that the poem was composed prior to June, 1900, when she started using the Gilman name.

Child Labor [no. 2]

This poem was originally published in *Forerunner* 1 (December 1909): 10.

En Banc

This poem was originally published in *Impress* 19 (January 1895): 5.

A Psalm of Lives

This poem was originally published in the *Saturday Review of Literature* (26 November 1927): 358.

The War-Skunk

In her diary entry for Wednesday, 7 October 1891, Gilman noted writing "The War-Skunk" and added that it was "apropos of Ambrose Bierce of the [San Francisco] *Examiner*." Bierce had often made disparaging remarks about the Pacific Coast Women's Press Association, of which Gilman was a member, in the early 1890s. Gilman also had contempt for William Randolph Hearst and his publishing empire after the Hearst-owned *Examiner* published a full-page expose of her impending divorce in February, 1893.

The Yellow Reporter

Gilman dated this poem 30 October 1906 and originally titled it "Shame." She wrote "The Yellow Reporter" above the original title, apparently to describe the subject matter. In her hand-written list of poems for inclusion, however, she identified the poem as "The Yellow Reporter."

I Would Fain Die a Dry Death

This poem was originally published in the *Independent*, 14 June 1906, 1401.

How About The Man?

1. American writer and politician Upton Sinclair (1878–1968) is best known for his novel, *The Jungle* (1906), a polemical tract attacking the primitive working conditions in the Chicago stockyards at the turn of the century.

A Diet Undesired

This poem was originally published in *Forerunner* 2 (June 1911): 153.

We Eat at Home

This poem was originally published in *Forerunner* 1 (July 1910): 16.

Special Dry Toast

This poem was originally published in *Forerunner* 6 (June 1915): 149.

Why? To the United States of America, 1915—1916

This poem was originally published in *Forerunner* 7 (January 1916): 5.

On Germany

Gilman appended the following handwritten note at the bottom of the typescript: "Just after the war. O if we had only had the sense to march three armies into Berlin!"

The Internationalist

This poem was originally published in *Life* 15 (March 1923): 13.

An Army With Banners

This poem was originally published in *Forerunner* 5 (August 1914): 213.

Pikers

This poem was originally published in the *New York Times*, 31 October 1920, section 7, 1:1–2. Gilman added the following parenthetical note after the title: "Published just before the Presidential Election of 1920, U.S.A."

Women of 1920

This poem was originally published in the New York *World*, 2 November 1920, 14:3. Gilman added the following note after the title: "These and 'Pikers' my special political efforts."

More Females of the Species

This poem was originally published in *Forerunner* 2 (December 1911): 318.

The Gunman

This poem was originally published in *Forerunner* 6 (January 1915): 11.

High Sovereignty

This poem was originally published in the *Independent*, 12 July 1906, 79.

This is a Lady's Hat

This poem was originally published in *Forerunner* 5 (April 1914): 92.

Big hats—Women's—At Base Ball!

Gilman added a handwritten note that this poem was written "about 1910."

Her Hat Still With Us

Gilman added a handwritten note that this poem was written "about 1910."

Mrs. Noah

This poem was originally published in *Forerunner* 2 (October 1911): 263. Gilman added the following handwritten note to the poem: "days of the "hobble skirt."

The Cripple

This poem was originally published in *Forerunner* 1 (March 1910): 26.

A Protest

This poem was originally published in *Appeal to Reason*, 24 (March 1900): 3. Gilman added the following handwritten note to the poem: "Good when written in the [18]90s."

The Speaker's Sin

This poem was originally published in the *Woman's Journal* 17 (November 1900): 366, under the title, "The Ladies' Sin." It was reprinted in *The Living of Charlotte Perkins Gilman*, 279–80.

The Love of Human Kind

This poem was originally published in the *Women's Journal* 5 (March 1904): 74.

Another Creed

This poem was originally published in *In This Our World*, 4th ed., 113–114. Gilman dated the poem 3 January 1897.

The Fool Killer

This poem was originally published in the *Woman's Journal*, 4 (May 1904): 74.

Kitchen Women

This poem was originally published in the *Woman's Journal* 5 (November 1904): 354.

The Housewife

This poem was originally published in *Forerunner* 1 (September 1910): 18.

The Proposal

This poem was originally published in the *Woman's Journal* 22 (October 1904): 338.

Ode to the Cook

This poem was originally published in the *Woman's Journal* 30 (January 1904): 34.

The Eternal Mother to the Bachelor Maid

This poem was originally published in the *Woman's Journal* 20 (August 1904): 266.

Two Callings

This poem was originally published in Gilman's non-fiction work, *The Home*, vii–xi.

Limiting Life

This poem was originally published in *Forerunner* 5 (August 1914): 222.

A Vandal

This poem was originally published in *Forerunner* 3 (May 1912): 121.

The Real Religion

This poem was originally published in *Forerunner* 5 (May 1914): 121.

A Central Sun

This poem was originally published in *Forerunner* 1 (January 1910): i.

The Rabbit, the Rhinoceros and I

This poem was originally published in *Forerunner* 3 (March 1912): 83.

The Oyster & The Starfish

This poem was originally published in the *Forum* 74 (October 1925): 629.

The Fatalist and The Sailorman

Gilman added the following note to the poem: "unpublished—be sure it goes in!"

The Weeping Nautilus

This poem originally appeared under the title "Another Conservative" in the *Pacific Monthly* 3 (March 1891): 105–06.

The Daily Squid

This poem was originally published in *Forerunner* 6 (August 1915): 206.

Some Nordics

This poem was originally published in *American Hebrew*, 18 August 1933, 203.

Tree & Sun

Gilman added a note that this poem was written on 22 June 1918.

Why Nature Laughs

This poem was originally published in the *Pacific Monthly* 2 (November 1890): 184.

Twigs

This poem was originally published in *Life*, 21 February 1924, 4.

The Front Wave

This poem was originally published in the *Saturday Review of Literature* (7 January 1933): 372.

Queer People

This poem was originally published in *Cosmopolitan* 27 (June 1899): 172.

The Earth, The World, and I

This poem was originally published in *Cosmopolitan* 28 (February 1900): 383–384.

The Flag of Peace

This poem was originally published in *Forerunner* 2 (September 1911): 234.

Song for the World's Flag

This poem was originally published in *Forerunner* 5 (December 1914): 321.

State Sovereignty

Gilman added the following note to the manuscript copy of the poem: "When Cal[ifornia]. was talking big about state sovereignty and making Japan angry."

1. Gilman held racist views throughout her life. See, for example, her essay, "A Suggestion on the Negro Problem" (1908), reprinted in Larry Ceplair's collection, *Charlotte Perkins Gilman: A Nonfiction Reader*, (Columbia University Press, 1992). She also occasionally used racist language and disparaging slang in her writing.

The Kingdom

This poem was originally published in *Forerunner* 1 (May 1910): 8–9.

Happiness

This poem was originally published in *Forerunner* 2 (November 1911): 287.

Begin Now

This poem was originally published in *Forerunner* 2 (October 1911): 260.

Thankfulness

An undated published clipping of this poem appears in Folder 190 of the Gilman Papers at the Schlesinger Library, Radcliffe College. Quoted by permission.

A Chant Royal

Gilman listed the title of the poem in her tentative table of contents as "The Day of Freedom. A Chant Royal." She added an explanatory note to the manuscript copy of the poem that reads, "A Chant Royal—to order—When Equal Suffrage was won." She also added a marginal note on the manuscript labeling each of the sections of the poem as follows: I. Her Slavery; II. Her Struggle; III. Her Opponents; IV. Her Progress; V. Her Triumph. She listed the date of composition as 11–13 March 1920.

Happy Day

This poem was originally published in *Woman's Journal* 6 (April 1912): 112. Gilman added the following notes to the manuscript copy of the poem: "To the tune of 'Dixie,'" and "got a $100.00 prize; written week of May 27th, 1911."

Noblesse Oblige

This poem was originally published in *American Fabian* 4 (April 1898): 7.

Where Women Meet

This poem was originally published in *Woman's Journal* 20 (February 1904): 58.

To the Indifferent Woman

This poem was originally published in *Woman's Journal* 27 (February 1904): 66.

One Girl of Many

Gilman included a parenthetical note on the manuscript copy of the poem that reads as follows: "It needs must be that offenses come, but woe unto *her* through whom that offense cometh." In *The Living of Charlotte Perkins Gilman*, Gilman wrote that the poem was "a defense of what was then termed the 'fallen' woman" (62). She also incorrectly identifies it as her first published poem. Her first published poem was actually "To D.G.," which appeared in the 20 May 1880 issue of the *New England Journal of Education*. Cf. note 25 of introduction, above. "One Girl of Many" was originally published in *Alpha* 1 (February 1884): 15.

The Departing Housemaid

This poem was originally published in *Twentieth Century Home* 1 (February 1904): 23.

The Past Parent & The Coming Child

This poem was originally published in *Woman's Journal* 12 (March 1904): 90, under the title, "Parent and Child."

Matriatism

This poem was originally published in *Forerunner* 5 (November 1914): 299.

Full Motherhood

This poem was originally published in *Forerunner* 6 (October 1915): 272.

To Mothers

This poem was originally published in *In This Our World*, 1st ed., 37–39.

Dark Ages

On the manuscript copy, Gilman titled the poem "Black Ages." In her note to Amy Wellington, however, she wrote that the "Woman Poems," from which "Dark Ages" is taken, were for her "to look over—see what might have been! There may be bits worth keeping—notably 'I Lived & Bore.' Might call it 'Dark Ages.'"

The Source

This poem was originally published in *Woman's Journal* 23 (April 1904): 122.

I am Human

This poem was originally published in *Woman's Journal* 16 (July 1904): 226.

Good Will

Gilman appended the following note to this poem: "1895. Leaving California, with twenty-five borrowed dollars, after seven years of my best work, kicked out, utter failure. And this is the way I felt. Written on train." Gilman reprinted part of the poem in *The Living of Charlotte Perkins Gilman*, 180.

The Coming Day

This poem is a revised and abbreviated version of "Good Will" (see above). "The Coming Day" originally appeared in *Woman's Journal* 28 (May 1904): 170.

This is the Year

This poem was originally published in *Forerunner* 2 (January 1911): 7.

Thoughts and Facts

This poem was originally published in *Forerunner* 3 (April 1912): 95.

The Human Law

This poem was originally published in *Forerunner* 3 (August 1912): 214–215.

The Purpose

This poem was originally published in *Woman's Journal* 12 (March 1904): 82.

The Primal Power

This poem was originally published in *Woman's Journal* 9 (April 1904): 114.

Two Prayers

This poem was originally published in *Forerunner* 1 (February 1910): i.

Whatever Is

This poem was originally published in *Cosmopolitan*, 37 (June 1904), 170.

Wings

This poem was originally published in *In This Our World*, 3rd ed., 116–117.

Worship

This poem was originally published in *Forerunner* 1 (November 1910): i.

The Artist

This poem was originally published in *Forerunner* 2 (May 1911): 126.

My View, 1881.

This poem was originally published in the Buffalo *Christian Advocate*, 17 January 1884, 1. Gilman added the following note to the manuscript copy of the poem: "(The house was on the north-west concern of Manning and Ives sts. in Providence. Mine was the west of two third floor windows.)"

Little Leafy Brothers

This poem was originally published in *Conservator* 19 (August 1908): 84–85. Gilman noted the date of composition of the poem as March 12–15, 1898.

In Alabama Woods

This poem was originally published in *Woman's Journal* 25 (June 1904): 202.

The Sphynx of Stone

Gilman dated the poem, "Chicago, 1896."

To Isadora Duncan

Gilman added the following marginal note on the handwritten manuscript of the poem: "Sent a copy to [Duncan] and she never even said thank you."

Out of Doors

This poem was originally published in *Cosmopolitan* 39 (May 1905): 2–3.

The Sands

This poem was originally published in *Forerunner* 1 (March 1910): i.

On A Tub of Butter, Christmas 1882

Gilman added the following notes to the manuscript copy of the poem: "To a friend who gave me a tub of butter. Please save." A second note was addressed to Amy Wellington: "Just to amuse you, Amy. It is really 'poetic'—in spots. Copied by my mother." Gilman's diary entry for 19 December 1882, indicates that the tub of butter was from her close Providence friend Ada Blake.

To Mary Shaw On Her Birthday, 1922

Gilman added the following note to the poem: "'occasional' verse. A 'dinner' was given her. I read this."

For A Guest Book

Gilman added the following notes to the manuscript copy of the poem: "Why not say 'For Martha Bruer's Guest Book'—I think she'd like it." Gilman added another note at the bottom of the manuscript: "Why not put it in—so entitled. It's a nice one."

Lecture Verse [no. 1]

Gilman added the following note to the manuscript copy of this poem: "For address, "Our Place Today," given before the Ebell Club, Oakland, Calif, Mon., April 20th, 1891."

Lecture Verse [no. 2]

Gilman added a note at the top of this poem that it was delivered at the "Opening of Ladies Class in Biography, November 1st, 1889."

Mer-Songs

Gilman added a note to the manuscript copy of the Mer-Song collection that reads as follows: "Child verse. Make a fine illustrated Xmas book with the other loose [child verses] maybe. My son-in-law spoke of doing it once!"

The Bad Little Coo-Bird

Gilman reprinted "The Bad Little Coo-Bird" in *The Living of Charlotte Perkins Gil-*

man (160–61) with the following comment about her use of the poem with her daughter, Katharine, in the early 1890s: "One of our morning games I put quite literally in verse, and the editor who published it urged that I give myself to the writing of children's verse—said I had a special talent for it" (161). To the manuscript copy of the poem she added, "Katharine & I used to play this in our bed—Pasadena—1890."

A Walk, Walk, Walk

This poem was originally published in *Forerunner* 1 (February 1910): 25.

Aunt Eliza

This poem, written in collaboration with another person composing alternate lines, was originally published in *Forerunner* 1 (March 1910): 25.

A Dream of Gold

This poem, written in collaboration with Gilman's life-long friend, Martha A. Luther, was originally published in *Forerunner* 4 (February 1913): 45. Gilman added the following note to the manuscript copy of this poem: "One of the best I ever took part in—a fine sestina done by Martha L. Lane of Hingham Mass. & C. P. Gilman, in prompt alternate lines."

The Melancholy Rabbit

This poem was originally published in *Forerunner* 1 (January 1910): 30.

A Use of Memory

This poem was originally published in *Woman's Journal* 18 (December 1886): 406.

Motion

This poem was originally published in *Woman's Journal* 2 (July 1904): 210.

Closed Doors

This poem was originally published in *Scribner's* 24 (November 1898): 548.

Little flutters of California beauty

Gilman added the following note to these poems: "California always makes me sing— just spatters, these."

The Grapevine

"The Grapevine," dated March, 1935, is Gilman's last-known verse. Her daughter Katharine added the following note to the manuscript copy of the poem: "Written 1935 on way back to Pasadena from a motor trip to see the wild flowers with the Robie Stevens family—near the 'grapevine.' K.S.C." In a letter to Gilman dated 5 August 1935, Amy Wellington promised to "place 'The Grapevine' with the other California verses."

Santa Barbara to San Jose

Gilman added the following note of instruction, apparently to Amy Wellington: "Be sure this goes [in]—I love it." She dated the poem 17 March 1922. Another slightly altered version titled "California Colors," also dated 17 March 1922, follows.

California Colors

This poem was originally published in *Forerunner* 6 (April 1915): 93.

Select Bibliography

Works by Charlotte Perkins Gilman

Charlotte Perkins Gilman: A Nonfiction Reader. Edited by Larry Ceplair. New York: Columbia University Press, 1992.

Charlotte Perkins Gilman Reader. Edited with an introduction by Ann J. Lane. New York: Pantheon, 1980.

Concerning Children. Boston: Small, Maynard & Co., 1901.

The Diaries of Charlotte Perkins Gilman. Edited with an introduction by Denise D. Knight. Charlottesville: University Press of Virginia, 1994.

Forerunner 1–7 (1909–16). Reprint, with an introduction by Madeleine B. Stern. New York: Greenwood, 1968.

Herland. Serialized in *Forerunner* 6 (1915). Reprint, with an introduction by Ann J. Lane. New York: Pantheon, 1979.

His Religion and Hers: A Study of the Faith of Our Fathers and the Work of Our Mothers. New York: Century Co. 1923.

The Home: Its Work and Influence. New York: McClure, Phillips & Co., 1903.

Human Work. New York: McClure, Phillips & Co., 1904.

In This Our World. Oakland: McCombs & Vaughn, 1893. 3d. ed. Boston: Small, Maynard & Co., 1898. Reprint. New York: Arno, 1974.

The Living of Charlotte Perkins Gilman: An Autobiography. Foreword by Zona Gale. New York: Appleton-Century, 1935. Reprint, with an introduction by Ann J. Lane. Madison: University of Wisconsin Press, 1990.

The Man-Made World, or, Our Androcentric Culture.Forerunner 1 (1909–10). Reprint. New York: Charlton Co., 1911.

Women and Economics: A Study of the Economic Relation Between Men and Women as a Factor in Social Evolution. Boston: Small, Maynard & Co., 1898. Reprint, with introduction by Carl Degler. New York: Harper & Row, 1966.

The Yellow Wallpaper. Boston: Small, Maynard & Co., 1899. Reprint, with an afterword by Elaine Hedges. Old Westbury: Feminist Press, 1973.

The Yellow Wall-Paper and Selected Stories of Charlotte Perkins Gilman, Edited with an introduction by Denise D. Knight. Newark: University of Delaware Press, 1994.

Secondary Readings

Allen, Polly Wynn. *Building Domestic Liberty: Charlotte Perkins Gilman's Architectural Feminism.* Amherst: University of Massachusetts Press, 1988.

Degler, Carl N. "Charlotte Perkins Gilman on the Theory and Practice of Feminism." *American Quarterly* 8 (Spring 1956), 21–39.

Hill, Mary A. *Charlotte Perkins Gilman: The Making of a Radical Feminist 1860–1896.* Philadelphia: Temple University Press, 1980.

———. *Endure: The Diaries of Charles Walter Stetson.* Philadelphia: Temple University Press, 1985.

Howe, Harriet. "Charlotte Perkins Gilman—As I Knew Her." *Equal Rights: Independent Feminist Weekly* 5 (September 1936): 211–16.

Karpinski, Joanne B. *Critical Essays on Charlotte Perkins Gilman.* Boston: G. K. Hall, 1992.

Kessler, Carol Farley, "Brittle Jars and Bitter Jangles: Light Verse by Charlotte Perkins Gilman," *Regionalism and the Female Imagination* 4 (Winter 1979); repr. in *Charlotte Perkins Gilman: The Woman and Her Work,* ed. Sheryl L. Meyering (Ann Arbor: UMI Research Press, 1989), 133–43.

Knight, Denise D. "Charlotte Perkins Gilman's Forgotten First Publication," in *ANQ: A Quarterly Journal of Short Articles, Notes, and Reviews* 7.4 (October 1994): 223–25.

———. "'With the first grass-blade': Whitman's Influence on the Poetry of Charlotte Perkins Gilman," in *Walt Whitman Quarterly Review* (Summer 1993): 18–29.

Lane, Ann J., *To Herland and Beyond: The Life and Work of Charlotte Perkins Gilman.* New York: Pantheon, 1980.

Meyering, Sheryl L., ed. *Charlotte Perkins Gilman: The Woman and Her Work.* Foreword by Cathy N. Davidson. Ann Arbor: UMI Research Press, 1989.

Scharnhorst, Gary. *Charlotte Perkins Gilman.* Boston: Twayne, 1985.

———. *Charlotte Perkins Gilman: A Bibliography.* Metuchen: Scarecrow, 1985.

———. "Reconstructing *Here Also*: On the Later Poetry of Charlotte Perkins Gilman," in *Critical Essays on Charlotte Perkins Gilman,* ed. Joanne Karpinski. New York: G. K. Hall, 1992, 249–268.

Walker, Cheryl, ed. *American Women Poets of the Nineteenth Century: An Anthology.* New Brunswick: Rutgers University Press, 1992.

Wellington, Amy, "Charlotte Perkins Gilman," from *Women Have Told: Studies in the Feminist Tradition.* Boston: Little, Brown, 1930, 115–131.